Happy and successful relationships are built on intimacy, truth, and a fulfilling sex life. A widely recognized writer, TV personality, and experienced sex therapist, Mary Jo Rapini, and, a nationally recognized urologist, Mohit Khera MD, who specializes in treating sexual dysfunction, have joined together to produce a guide book for couples seeking to improve their marriage.

RE-COUPLING*

A Couple's 4-step Guide to Greater Intimacy and Better Sex

by

Mary Jo Rapini, L.P.C.

and

Mohit Khera, M.D., M.B.A., M.P.H.

* Definition: to couple or join again

M⊙tivational PRESS®

LEADERS IN GLOBAL PUBLISHING

Published by Motivational Press, Inc.
1777 Aurora Road
Melbourne, Florida, 32935
www.MotivationalPress.com

Manufactured in the United States of America.

ISBN: 978-1-62865-182-9

The authors would like to thank Carolyn Schum, MA, for her skillful editing and for the patience and perseverance that she brought to this endeavor.

Contents

Forward

As a general internal medicine physician and a practitioner of male and female sexual medicine, I am always searching for and grateful to find resources for my patient's that are "general" and apply to everyone. Yet at the same time, I hope to offer specialized information, particularly about male and female sexuality, that addresses specific questions and offers detailed, practical advice. This guide does an excellent job of meeting the needs of couples seeking to enhance intimacy and improve their sexual relationship.

Re-Coupling: A Couple's 4-Step Guide to Greater Intimacy and Better Sex is a comprehensible, comprehensive, and encompasses both the male and the female perspective, as well as the couple's integrated point of view. Using interesting cases and textboxes with key messages, the information is personalized and amplified for the reader. The book focuses on rejuvenation of sexuality in long term relationships, highlighting the importance of commitment, novelty, intimacy, and love.

The authors' 4-Step model fits together clearly and elegantly, and each step builds nicely on the previous component(s). Step 1 recommends improving communication skills between partners both in and out of the bedroom. They emphasize that effective communication between partners about their relationship in general and about sex in particular is the foundation for successful intimacy and enhanced sexuality.

Step 2 provides a succinct, clear, and thorough explanation about the biological and psychological/emotional factors that contribute to sexual function and dysfunction. The text clearly explains the key organic issues and their treatment for both men and women, so both members of the couple can be educated. The book addresses important biological concerns such as libido, the role of testosterone for men and women in sexual desire, causes and treatment options for erectile dysfunction, the contribution and management of chronic medical conditions such as chronic obstructive pulmonary disease, penile disorders such as Peyronie's Disease, and changes in sexual response with aging. Additionally, the book discusses the impact of lifestyle modification such as obesity, body image, stress, and exercise, emphasizing the positive benefits of lifestyle changes on sexuality.

Sexual dysfunction is presented as a couples issue; the authors emphasize the importance of treating both partners simultaneously, explaining that improvements in one partner's sexual function will likely lead to enhancement of the other's sexual experience. The authors also articulate differences in male and female response and offer an alternate model for understanding female sexuality that centers emotional intimacy as a significant motivation, rather than spontaneous desire for sex. For female sexual dysfunction the authors present an easy to understand algorithm that outlines the management of female sexual dysfunction, using a stepwise approach: identification, education, modification, and medical/surgical therapy.

In Step 3 the couple is offered guidance about how to re-establish intimacy and re-energize contact. This section directs the couple to resolve underlying relationship issues, reawaken romance, and manage boredom, offering suggestions such as communication about preferences, sex toys, and novelty. The authors recommend fun, laughter, and a "cuddle plan" for renewing the intimate bonds and rekindling the sexual relationship.

The final Step 4 titled, "Go – For Better Sex," boldly endorses the benefits of orgasm and techniques for improving orgasmic response in men and women. The text provides straightforward information about technique, masturbation, vibrators, and lubricants. It also thoughtfully articulates approaches to "reinventing" a relationship in the face of chronic illness and "recovering" sexuality after a cancer diagnosis and treatment. The final message of this all-inclusive manual celebrates the value of sexual intimacy and its salutary effect on overall health.

Sharon J. Parish, MD

Professor of Medicine in Clinical Psychiatry,

Weill Cornell Medical College

President, International Society for the Study of Women's Sexual Health

Introduction

Having sex is the most intimate experience a person can have with another human being. The expression of sex is distorted in magazines, TV, Internet, and movies, but it remains sacred and necessary if couples are to feel connected and content in their relationships.

Although I have been an intimacy, sex psychotherapist for more than 15 years, I was surprised by a recent newspaper article reporting that as many as 80% of couples who suffer from a sexual problem learn to live with it. They don't seek help, and they don't see a possibility of improvement. Many times what keeps them immobilized is that the prospect of talking to a health care professional fills them with fear. With this in mind, I contacted my colleague Dr. Mohit Khera (a Urologist) and asked him to help me address this problem. We decided that perhaps we could reach these troubled couples with a useful guidebook.

For several years Dr. Khera and I have worked as a team, seeing patients with sexual dysfunction and working with their partners as well. We have worked with young couples, older couples, gay couples, and couples struggling with serious illnesses such as cancer. We have learned that sex issues don't ever happen in a vacuum. Sexual dysfunction is a couple's disease and equally affects both partners. It is for this reason that we urge readers to work through this book as a couple.

In our practices Dr. Khera and I refer patients to each other. We may sometimes make use of questionnaires and check lists, and we have included some of them or websites where they can be found for your use. You are the ones who must take the first steps to become a couple again.

Our goal is to offer a 4-step guide to lead both you and your partner to a greater understanding of your own expressions of intimacy and sex. Many things hold couples together, and we think that good sex is one of them.

We hope that our 4-step approach offers a helpful guide. We wish you success.

Mary Jo Rapini

Before I begin treatment of a couple seeking help for a marriage that is in trouble, I ask them to commit to working together for a year to save their relationship. Sometimes one party has already decided on divorce, but if they agree to give it a try, we proceed to work through the following 4 steps.

STEP 1: IMPROVE COMMUNICATION

Step 1 seems self-evident, but it is not easy. Couples drift apart for many reasons, and the first step is to work on communication skills and find the causes of this separation.

The Importance of Communication in Your Relationship

When couples come to see me complaining that they haven't had sex in several months, there generally is palpable tension between them. They often are in a panic-stricken search for the reasons why. When sex is going well, it is 10% of the relationship. However, when sex isn't going well, it can become 90% of the relationship. And couples seldom know how to communicate about any problems, much less their sexual problems.

Winning an Argument Doesn't Mean You Communicate Well

I would never marry someone with whom I couldn't argue. In fact, studies have shown that unhappy married couples don't fight any more than happy ones, but the manner in which they fight is much different. Arguing is an important aspect of a relationship. It helps clear the air, establish boundaries, and reveal points of view. Arguing also helps couples understand each other's vulnerabilities and uncovers their "hot buttons." The longer happily married couples are together, the less they push those hot buttons. They understand that those reactions won't change, and that when those buttons are pushed, "holy hell" can break out. In fact, I have observed that when older couples are pushing each other's hot buttons, they usually are doing it on purpose because their needs aren't being met and they are angry with one another.

Early in their marriage, a couple may not have a healthy respect for those hot buttons. Because they are in the honeymoon phase, they want to be totally transparent and are convinced that their love can disarm the hot buttons, allowing them to get to the bottom of the problem. It the office it is difficult to distract them or move them toward another area. They want to go for those buttons, analyze them, take them apart and cool them down. Very rarely is this effective, and this is when couples learn that there is a winner and a loser in these arguments. Many times, the partner who wins the argument loses the game, because hurtful things are said in the heat of the moment. This pattern of arguing to win at all costs rather than trying to understand is at the heart of the problems of many couples, although neither partner ever tells me this. They tell me they have a controlling partner, someone who cannot talk to them without arguing, or that they don't talk any more as a couple. If partners don't communicate verbally, it isn't long before one of the partners starts withdrawing physically, and once this happens, the marriage is in trouble.

Healthy communication requires patience, understanding. and listening. When a marriage is stressed, those three aspects are ignored and replaced with lecturing, yelling, and shutting down. People who believe they are great communicators often are great only at winning the argument.

Interestingly, their ways of communicating are the first characteristics that I observe when I meet a new couple; yet many of us don't think about our communication style until we can no longer communicate with our partners.

Lilly and Robert were a typical example. When they entered the room they sat as far apart as possible. She appeared ready to cry and he clearly didn't want to be there. Lilly says they have come because she feels that she has become invisible and she wants to know if there is any hope for their marriage. He is sullen and defensive, saying he is working hard to keep bread on the table and just wants to be left alone when he gets home. He spends the day trying to make other people feel "visible" and doesn't think he should have to worry about a wife whom he loves.

Lilly and Robert clearly had not discussed their feelings with each other, and what communication had occurred had been negative rather than positive.

Changing your communication style is the quickest way to tighten up your marriage. You don't need a therapist for this   You just need to get your partner's attention at a quiet time and say that you want to work on communicating better with each other.. As is usually true, changing yourself first is the best way to get the ball rolling.

Suggestions for returning communication to your marriage

1   *Talking louder never helps. When you are talking to your partner, make a conscious effort to lower your voice. It's often true that what your partner is <u>hearing</u> is not what you are <u>saying</u>.*   •

2   *Try saying one sentence to your partner's three. This one simple tactic will help you listen more than you talk. There will be more space in the conversation, which will mean more time to think before talking.*

3   *Solution of most problems is a process. Don't be in a rush to solve or get to the bottom of anything. The longer you are married the more you will understand that thinking there is a bottom to anything is magical thinking.*

4   *When you are communicating well, make note of it aloud and tell your partner how much you enjoyed the conversation. Both men and women need to be appreciated by their partners.*

Talking about sex with your partner

The number of my patients who are unhappy with their sex lives is astounding. Many of these couples have been married for five, ten, or twenty years, and they report that they are awkward and dissatisfied with the type and frequency of sex they have. Our society leads us to believe that it is women, not men, who are more uncomfortable when talking about sex, but, in my experience, this isn't true. Men are usually the ones who initiate counseling when they are feeling emotionally distressed about the sex in their relationship. Some of the discomfort comes from a sex life that has never been satisfying, and one partner is afraid of hurting the other by bringing it up. Couples often grow distant physically and become involved with their kids, personal interests, and work, and then stop having sex. Suddenly, when the kids are gone; their career goals have changed; they have more time, and they may find themselves sitting on the sofa with their spouses watching the news and wondering, "Is this all there is?" They miss the closeness, the excitement, and the pleasure that sex brought them.

A number of popular books offer advice and validation for the person who misses and wants sex, but has a partner unwilling to participate. However, what do you do when you have been an equal participant in letting your sex life grow stale, and find yourself wondering how to get it back? When you haven't had sex for more than a year, how do you approach the issue without seeming to criticize or blame? Couples talk about sex frequently when dating and engaged. This conversation usually becomes less frequent the longer couples are married. Other issues, such as buying or redecorating a house, working, and having kids, replace sex talk. This is unfortunate because keeping an open dialogue about sex, what you like, and how much your partner pleases you, helps build a strong foundation for your marriage. Kids, houses, and work cause stress and lead to anxiety. Sex decreases anxiety, depression, and health issues and provides a sense of togetherness and well-being. This enhances a marriage and leads to its longevity.

The most difficult part of communicating with your partner about sex may be the decision about how to begin the conversation. Perhaps you could write a note asking, "Can we talk about how we can connect more sexually?" Put it in a place where your partner will see it. Then, without pressuring your partner, watch for the response. We all communicate, although not directly at times. Watch your partner's non-verbal behavior as he or she reads the note. **Avoid being accusing or passive, but be sure to state your desire to learn better ways to communicate sexually.** Below are a few other suggestions that may help you break the ice and have a good "sex talk."

Pillow Talk: 10 Tips For <u>Talking About</u> Sex

1. The bathtub is a wonderful place to have a conversation dealing with sex. It is warm, smells good, and you have face to face eye contact. It is difficult to feel defensive in the water. Usually bath time is time for you. Water is calming and familiar from our beginnings in the womb.

2. It is best to begin by telling your partner you miss him or her sexually. ask how they feel about sex and then listen. Complaining or demanding that your needs be met will make your partner withdraw. It is important to be aware of any resentment that may interfere with the desire to have sex. resentment can kill both the libido and relationship.

3. Start out by touching again. ask your partner where they like to be touched and then touch them. ask them for feedback.

4. You will have more success if you plan at least 15 minutes of each day to talk about your sex life.

5. Watching love stories or listening to music together while lying in bed or on the couch presents a wonderful way to begin the conversation in regards to your own sexual feelings.

6. Men place a lot of value on their ability to please their woman. Women should take note and express their pleasure openly.

7. Don't expect your partner to read your mind. If you don't like the way your partner touches you in a certain area of your body, guide them to an area that feels better.

8. Talk about how you feel about your body as you have changed through the years. You may have felt your partner didn't find you attractive, when it was simply a matter of awkwardness on your partner's part in being sexual after a long while without engaging.

9. Talking about the kids, the house, or work is not advisable when exploring your sexuality. talking about happy memories or silly things is much better. laughing makes sex talk easier and makes sex better.

10. If one partner has a stronger drive than the other, you can talk about the fact that sex is more than intercourse; it involves feeling loved and desired all the time, and that is important to all of us.

A healthy couple understands that at times one or the other of them is called upon to make a greater contribution to the relationship, and that this is actually healthy. Sometimes kids do take precedence. Jobs may be all-consuming for a while, as may be buying and decorating a new home. However, when other aspects of life become so consuming that you continually put sex on the back burner, you are jeopardizing the health of your marriage. Couples need to connect and enjoy one another sexually.

In a healthy marriage no one should ever have to apologize for desiring sex with a spouse. However, the way in which that need is communicated usually predicts if and when sex will happen. I would ask Lilly and Robert when they last had sex. Frequently one or the other partner won't remember. Or they will remember differently. I might ask whether they ever hold hands. Have a date night? Have a real vacation? I would ask how they communicate their feelings and needs and when either of them last did so? I would strongly suggest that they sit down in a quiet place and take the time to try to identify the reasons for the distance that has developed between them. **It is important for a couple to identify and deal with the causes of stress, depression, or distraction and to learn to discuss their feelings about sex.**

Sometimes I ask a couple to take the **PHQ9** to identify depression. (Appendix 1)

I also try to make them aware of some potential causes of stress or distraction. Sometimes stress has external causes. Your work contributes to it. Your financial situation contributes to it. The kids contribute to it. Sleepless nights contribute to it. Stress takes a toll on our sex lives. In my office, couple after couple come in and complain about not being able to have an orgasm. A couple may not be able to let go of thinking about an upcoming deadline or budget, or they are too fatigued to enjoy making love. Another couple, watching the clock, knowing they have to get up early, may be stressed because one partner still hasn't climaxed. "Will he/she ever finish?" Distractions and worry interfere with the couples' ability to enjoy a sexual pleasure. If this sounds familiar you are not alone. According to the *Journal of the American Medical Association,* nearly half of all women and one third of men experience sexual dysfunction, and stress is reported to be one of the most significant risk factors for difficulties with sexual desire, arousal, and orgasm.. That stress can come from a variety of sources including job loss, death of a loved one, child care, sleepless nights, and the stress of the holidays. To evaluate the stress in your life take a look at the list of stressors listed below.. If you discover that stress may be interfering with your desire for sex, perhaps you can identify the causes and examine the effects.

Are you Stressed?

A couple's Intimacy and well being may be affected when one or both partners are under stress, and the stress may be caused by good fortune as well as bad. Ask yourself whether you are being affected by any of the following stressors. Any stressor or emotional condition lasting for a period longer than two weeks should be taken seriously. A visit to your mental health provider or a trusted counselor will help alleviate stress.

- Death in the family
- Issues dealing with remodeling, building or buying of a home or property.
- New baby
- Children leaving home
- Responsibility for parents or siblings
- Problems or changes at work, including promotion or retirement
- Conflicts with a colleague or good friend
- Relocation (moves are stressful)
- Financial changes of any kind

If one partner has a problem, both partners have a problem, and the best way to solve it is for the couple to work together, seeking help together and communicating with each other.

Stress doesn't go away. We learn how to live with it and manage it. Using these simple tools may help.

Tips For Dealing With Stress

As an individual

1 **Learn to breathe in slowly and out even more slowly.** *Breathe in to the count of 4 and out to the count of 7. Do this 5 times before you take any action (more if you are prone to physical expression of anger).*

2 *Take* a quick run or fast walk.

3 take a nice hot bath with nice smelling bath gels (the olfactory center is known for helping to calm the body with scents such as lavender).

4 Whatever you do, try to calm down before talking or acting on your stress or anger. **Talk about it to each other when you aren't stressed.**

5 **Keep a Journal..** a journal is a "little psychotherapist" in your pocket. seriously, if you write down your thoughts you will be able to handle your own stressors because you will begin to understand what they are and what precipitates them.

6 **Reach out..** Pick up the phone and call someone who likes you! There's nothing like a voice on the other end of the line that is glad you are part of their life! Everyone has at least one person on their side at all times. When you are stressed, this is the time to call that person.

7 **Write down ideas for helping relieve the stress of your partner.** For example, if your partner is afraid of losing his or her job, speak softly, express your love "no matter what" and offer assurances that you can "work it out as a team."

As a couple

8 **Begin by taking turns initiating sex.** some individuals say they are stressed because their partner never initiates anything and they feel totally responsible for when and if sex happens. When you initiate it, you get to set the stage too. If you are more romantic, find nice candles, and turn on soft music to make your "sex time" romantic. taking turns challenges partners to give more thought to the love making. put sex on your schedule and begin by scheduling it once a week. If you schedule it only once a week chances are greater that you will succeed and also that you will not be too tired. also, when you set your goals lower and you achieve them, it is much easier to build in more frequency as you are both feeling successful.

9 **talk to your partner.** When couples get stressed they forget to communicate. they become irritable and terse. set aside 15 minutes per day with your phones and computers turned off to look at your partner and talk. make sure this conversation takes place at a time when you can say what you are feeling in a non critical/non blaming way.

10. When you are calm, sit down with your partner and **make plans to engage in one new behavior a week.** When you plan a new activity together you immediately alleviate some stress because you are working together. part of stress is feeling alone and totally responsible.

11. **plan something "fun" to do with your partner each week.** It can be as simple as sitting in a book store drinking coffee and reading magazines or as out-of-the-ordinary as a night in a hotel. stress makes us old and boring. It is okay to put your stress on hold and enjoy your partner once a week.

STEP 2 GET READY FOR SEX -- BOTH PHYSICALLY AND EMOTIONALLY

There is nothing wrong with not having a strong sex drive. Many couples have sex once a month and are happily married. The problem arises when one partner has a strong drive and the other partner doesn't. As they work out the problems in their daily lives, couples may have more time and probably will be more inclined to think about sex. They may well ask "How do we regain the desire that we used to share?"

When I next saw Lilly and Robert they had talked about their relationship, identified some of the causes of stress and failure to communicate, and had made some lifestyle changes. Now she's smiling and he's engaged. They have tried to be less demanding and more sympathetic. They have arranged their evening schedules so that each of them has an uninterrupted "30-minute time out" at least 3 times a week. They work together to get the children to bed (or take turns). They consult about the budget, get clearance before inviting guests etc....

Lilly and Robert were in a much better frame of mind than they had been whern I first saw them and they considered that they were communicating much better, but their sex lives had not changed. Lilly said she didn't ever feel "sexy" and Robert said he didn't spend much time thinking about sex. Yet, they both were bothered by the loss of the excitement that had been such a part of their earlier years together.

Loss of Desire Could Be a Medical Problem.

My suggestion to Lilly and Robert was that each of them consider the possiblity that loss of desire (low libido) could be treated by a physician, and I referred them to Dr. Khera for a physical examination while we continued to work on emotional issues that might affect their desire for sex.

What keeps couples from wanting sex?

In his office, Dr. Khera will obtain a detailed medical history and will talk to the couple about their sex drive . He may arrange for testing of testosterone levels in both partners and will give each of them a thorough physical examination.

He will define and discuss with the couple the meaning and some of the effects of low libido. He will explain that "When libido is low you no longer feel any desire or passion for sex. You may feel dead inside and no longer want to make the effort to enjoy sex with your partner. Both men and women can suffer from low libido. Many times couples become frustrated with low libido and, because of their inability to talk about it, each partner begins to think that the other is the problem. This description by actual patients seems to ring loud and clear with other patients."

A 42- year-old woman reported, "I never really want to have sex, but sometimes my husband gets so upset, that it's easier having it than not. When we have it, I always find myself lying there looking up at the ceiling thinking of lists and other things I must remember as he thrusts away. I tell myself this isn't normal, but where do I begin?"

A 48-year-old man said, "I don't know what happened. I used to want sex all the time, and my wife was always saying "NO." Now I find myself no longer wanting it with her. I can't get excited about waking up next to her; I don't feel anything. I'm not really excited about other women either. How did this happen, and what is causing it?"

Testosterone for Men: A significant factor in libido

Over the past 5 years, the sales of testosterone have grown rapidly. From 2005 to 2009, spending on testosterone jumped 115.5%, and the number of prescriptions filled increased by 64.5%. In the United States today, the increase in prescriptions for Testosterone is second only to the increase in use of diabetic medications, and the growth of the testosterone market has been reported to be 22% per year.

There are many reasons for the rapid growth of testosterone sales. We have an aging population with the number of U.S. men 65 and older increasing 2-3 times faster than the number of men younger than 65. Furthermore, recent data demonstrate an increased association between poor general health, and, possibly mortality, and low serum testosterone levels. Men with lower testosterone levels have been shown to die at an earlier age than men with normal testosterone levels. There is now less concern about the development of prostate cancer after use of testosterone, making it a more attractive treatment option. In fact, to date, there is no study showing an increased risk for developing prostate cancer after starting testosterone treatment. Finally, new drugs entering the testosterone market with increased promotion, marketing, and directto-consumer advertising, are also driving market growth.

Many patients have not heard of "male menopause," "andropause," or "hypogonadism." All of these terms refer to the same thing: low testosterone in men. Men lose roughly 1% of testosterone every year starting at about 30 years of age. In some men this loss is even faster because of environmental and physical conditions. More and more younger men seem to be suffering from low testosterone, and often this reduction seems to be related to stress. We know that stress increases cortisol levels, which can decrease testosterone levels.

It is not surprising that many older men experience the same signs and symptoms that women experience as they go through menopause. Men experience increased fat mass, decreased muscle mass, depression, sexual dysfunction, loss of sex drive, mood changes, and loss of energy. (Table 1) Many men don't realize they are going through andropause and that there is treatment available to help them.

The diagnosis of low testosterone involves checking the patient's blood testosterone level and also making sure that he has the signs and symptoms of low testosterone. One problem is that the signs and symptoms of low testosterone are non-specific and can be found in association with numerous other conditions. One of the most commonly used questionnaires to screen men for low testosterone is referred to as the **Androgen Deficiency in the Aging Male (ADAM) questionnaire**. (See: http://www.counseling-office.com/surveys/test_testosterone_deficiency.phtml) This questionnaire asks 10 simple questions and if the answer is "yes" to questions 1 or 7, or to any three questions, a man is said to test positive. Take a moment to see if you test positive on the ADAM questionnaire.

Our knowledge of how testosterone relates to certain conditions such as depression, diabetes, heart disease, prostate cancer, and infertility has increased significantly. However, many clinicians are unaware that low testosterone can lead to depressive symptoms and that treating men with testosterone can improve these symptoms. A recent study found that 12 months of testosterone treatment in depressed men resulted in an 88% reduction in moderately severe and severe depressive symptoms. In this study, patients already taking anti-depressants also had a significant improvement in depressive symptoms, suggesting a synergistic effect of anti-depressants and testosterone in men suffering from depression.

Patients with diabetes and heart disease are at a significantly increased risk of having low testosterone. Testosterone treatment has been shown to improve diabetes and heart disease. A recent prospective, randomized double-blinded study (TIMES 2 Study) of 220 men with type 2 diabetes found that 12 months of testosterone treatment resulted in improvements in blood sugar levels and cholesterol. Historically, the relationship between heart disease and testosterone replacement has been controversial. However, more studies now suggest a beneficial effect of testosterone in cardiovascular health. Men with low testosterone who were given testosterone treatment have been shown to have an improvement in blood pressure levels and reduction in size of the plaques in their arteries. While these studies are encouraging, more research is needed in this field.

When asked what they think about when testosterone is mentioned, most men say they think about body building, sex drive, or athletes who got into trouble abusing hormone medications. What patients don't realize is that testosterone is involved in far more than just body building and sex drive. Men need testosterone to make proteins in the liver, to make red blood cells, to improve bone health, and to help with sperm production, as well as to maintain cardiovascular health.

Despite persistent concerns, there are still no convincing data to indicate that giving testosterone to men increases their risk of developing prostate cancer. In fact, although TV commercials, in an abundance of caution, continue to warn about possible side effects, studies of testosterone in men with a history of prostate cancer have demonstrated no increased risk of prostate cancer progression or recurrence. A randomized placebo-controlled study to further assess the safety and efficacy of testosterone in these men is currently under way.

Testosterone replacement can lead to infertility, and men desiring to initiate a pregnancy in the future should be counseled appropriately before initiating testosterone therapy. In these patients, there are ways to raise testosterone levels without causing infertility, but this usually involves pills or injections.

Testosterone Supplementation for Women

Perhaps surprising to some is that it may be the woman with low testosterone levels affecting libido.

Myths about testosterone and women: Myths and misconceptions patients have about testosterone and its effects on women are amazing. Many patients are still concerned about certain cancers such as breast cancer, ovarian cancer, or endometrial cancer. Currently there is no evidence to indicate that an increase in testosterone results in an increased risk of any of these cancers. In fact, some studies have shown that testosterone may reduce the risk of breast cancer in post menopausal women. There are also no data to suggest that higher levels of testosterone cause an increased risk of cardiovascular events. The transgender population have provided some of the best data we have as women underwent sex changes to become men. These women received 10 times the testosterone that most women have naturally, and experienced no increase in cases of cancer or cardiovascular events.

An internet search of "testosterone and women" will bring up many interesting associations of testosterone and women, most of which are not true. For example, there are reports that "testosterone may make women nicer" and that "women with higher testosterone are more likely to have sons." One article reported that testosterone may guide a woman's career path. This study showed that women with higher testosterone levels were more likely to take risks and choose a career in finance. Clearly, there is much more to learn about testosterone and how it affects women.

Although testosterone supplementation for women is not currently FDA-approved, many women in the US with low testosterone are being treated with off-label testosterone supplementation. The most common reason for this testosterone supplementation is low sexual desire. An estimated 43% of women in the United States suffer from low sexual desire. Testosterone supplementation has also been shown to improve sexual arousal, orgasmic function, and overall sexual satisfaction in women, but this treatment is not for everyone. It is important to understand the different causes of low testosterone in women and how to diagnose and treat this condition.

While estrogen has been shown to help improve a woman's desire for sex, testosterone is actually the main driver behind her sexual desire. The best evidence is that when a woman ovulates, releasing an egg for fertilization, for a period of roughly 12-24 hours she also has a surge of testosterone, which is nature's way of increasing her sexual desire during this time and increasing her chances for pregnancy. Numerous studies have demonstrated significant improvements in a woman's libido after initiation of testosterone replacement therapy. Several studies have also demonstrated the beneficial effect of combining testosterone and estrogen in women. These studies have found that sexual desire, sexual satisfaction, and frequency of sex in women taking hormonal therapy were improved significantly by a combination of estrogen and testosterone therapy compared to therapy with either estrogen or testosterone alone. It should be noted, however, that it can take approximately 3 months for the sexual benefits of testosterone therapy to become noticeable.

Diagnosis of Low Testosterone in Women

There are many signs and symptoms of low testosterone in women. A woman requires roughly 5 to10% of a man's daily dose of testosterone, or roughly 0.25 mg per day.

Signs of low testosterone in women include decreased lean body mass, increased body fat, thinning or loss of pubic hair, and osteopenia or osteoporosis. Symptoms of actual testosterone deficiency in women include a significant decline in sexual motivation and libido, persistent unexplained fatigue or lack of energy, and a lack of sense of well being. Women need far less testosterone than men.

Treatment for Low Testosterone in Women

To date, no forms of testosterone replacement therapy are FDA-approved in the United States for the treatment of low libido in women. Forms of testosterone supplementation include pellets placed under the skin, gels and patches, compounded creams, and testosterone injections. Currently testosterone patches are available throughout Europe (Intrinsa™, Proctor and Gamble) and are applied 2-3 times per week. Testosterone gels and creams are now gaining favor because they are associated with less skin irritation than the patches. Finally, testosterone pellets, which need to be changed every 4-6 months, have been used successfully.

Adverse effects of testosterone replacement therapy in women

Increased testosterone levels in women can cause side effects such as acne (6%), growth of unwanted hair (5.7%), hair loss (3.2%), and deepening of the voice (2.5%). However, stopping testosterone has been shown to reverse these adverse effects in most patients.

Testosterone Levels Are not the Only Facators In Women's Desire For Sex.

Among factors that affect women specifically are medications, depression, lack of sleep, and poor body image

- **Medications.** Birth control pills. That's right. For women, the very pill that prevents pregnancy so that they don't have to worry about an unwanted pregnancy can also cause low libido. Ovaries make hormones as well as eggs, and when they're put to rest for several weeks each month, hormone levels in the body drop. Another problem is that the pill causes the body to produce a protein called sex hormone binding globulin (SHBG), which binds itself to sex hormones, in particular testosterone, essentially sucking them up. Testosterone plays a role in vaginal blood flow and sensitivity in the opening of the vagina, so lower levels of this hormone can lead to sexual problems. Many women who quit the pill still struggle with their libido. Research has shown that the SHBG protein production can continue to be higher in former pill users than in non-pill users. Although this isn't a common occurrence, women who are affected by it, will need to get help.

What you can do? See a physician and get another type of birth control that can provide protection from pregnancy without affecting libido.

- **Breast feeding and child birth.** Having a baby is one of the greatest joys a couple can experience. However, it can dampen libido for both partners. Hormones changing quickly, fatigue, stress, and lack of sleep are all experienced, as is postpartum depression.

What you can do. The first rule is that if you are depressed after the birth of your baby, you should seek medical attention. This does not mean you are a bad mom; it means that your hormones are affecting your brain and that you will benefit from talking to your physician and, possibly, from receiving medication. This is not only for the sake of your sex drive; it is for your life as well as your baby's. Terrible things can happen when a woman has postpartum depression that is not dealt with. Secondly, try not to focus on sex; try to focus on communicating, cuddling, and being close to your partner. Time is the great healer with loss of libido after a baby and during breast feeding. The more connected you feel to your partner the more likely you are to begin feeling amorous again after childbirth.

- **Lack of sleep**. This seems like an obvious libido killer but most of us don't think of it. If you are working 12-hour shifts, or staying up with a baby, or getting less than 6 hours of sleep each night, this is not only unhealthy but is a killer for your sex life.

What can you do? Stop being a super man or a super mom. Your body needs to restore itself and so do your emotions. It is not selfish to demand your sleep; it is taking care of yourself. If you are a new parent, or a notso-new parent who is not getting sleep, sit down and talk to your partner and schedule sleep into your schedule. If you have to hire a housekeeper or babysitter or go to a hotel to sleep, do it. It will be money well invested. Lack of sleep can cause irritability, increased fighting, and resentment. Commit to yourself and your relationship. Fatigue is a killer in more ways than to your sex life.

Other Physical Problems: What keeps couples from Having sex?

Sometimes the problem is not lack of desire (low libido) but a physical inability such as erectile dysfunction or a problem such as pain during intercourse.

SEXUAL DYSFUNCTION IN MEN: "I WANT TO HAVE SEX BUT CAN'T"

Understanding the Anatomy

There are two main functions of the penis: to urinate and to have sex. The penis is made up of 3 "tubes." There are two tubes on top and one tube on the bottom. The end result is the appearance of an upside down triangle. The top two tubes, called "cavernosal bodies," are responsible for an erection. The bottom tube is called the "urethra" and is responsible for removing urine from the bladder. The head of the penis is called the glans. The glans does not become as hard as the shaft of the penis during an erection.. There are muscles surrounding the entire urethra and these muscles are responsible for squeezing when a man has an orgasm. The squeezing of these muscles allows the semen to make its way out of the penis. The penis is a very cleverly engineered system. The blood comes in through the center of the cavernosal bodies, and the blood leaves from the sides of the cavernosal bodies. As more blood comes in, it shuts off the valves that allow blood to go out. Thus the more blood that comes in, the less blood goes out, and the net result is an erection. The concept of an erection is very simple: more blood needs to come in and less blood to go out in order for a man to have an erection. The problem is that as men get older, the valves become more and more difficult to shut off . Some men develop something called "venous leak." The blood comes out too fast from the penis. These men will tell you "Doc, I can get the erection, but I just can't maintain it." The best way to treat this problem is either to increase the rate at which the blood comes into the penis or to decrease the rate at which the blood leaves the penis. The easiest way to stop the blood from leaving is to use a penile restriction band. This is a band placed at the base of the penis so that it prevents the blood from leaving.

Receiving a diagnosis of erectile dysfunction is an opportunity for better sex

Frequently, we see couples who worry about erectile dysfunction when the changes they are experiencing are completely normal. Aging, stress, and intimacy conflicts can all keep a man from achieving an erection. Although drugs, such as Viagra and Cialis, have made it easier to achieve an erection, these medications may mask a problem that shouldn't be ignored.

Many people medicate a symptom, such as an inability to achieve an erection, before understanding the underlying problem. Medical illnesses, such as diabetes, vascular disease, or urological and neurological conditions, can also cause erectile dysfunction. Heavy smokers and drinkers may suffer extensive damage to the small blood vessels, which include those in the penis. For many men, erectile dysfunction includes a combination of physical and psychological factors. If you address your diabetes, but don't get help with the resentment you feel toward your partner, the penis is not going to perform to your satisfaction no matter what medication you use. Men are dating later in life and, with dating, there is pressure to perform. It is easy to become panicked or anxious when the penis doesn't perform as expected. Some common worries that may be signs of aging, anxiety, stress, and intimacy conflict rather than of actual erectile dysfunction are the following:

- You no longer get an erection when just thinking about sex or seeing your partner in a seductive pose. For men over 40, this is quite common from time to time.
- You need direct stimulation to get erect.
- It takes longer for you to achieve an erection (this may be more pleasing to your partner).
- Your erection is not as hard as it was when you were a teen or in your early twenties.
- You need more recovery time after ejaculation. (This changes with each passing year.) And after ejaculation, your erection subsides much more quickly than it did when you were younger.

A man's partner plays an important role if he is worried about erectile dysfunction. Reminding him that she loves him and still enjoys intimacy with him helps reassure him that he is still her lover and able to please her. Complaining that "all he thinks about is sex" is not only thoughtless, but sends him the direct message that he is being silly or superficial to be so concerned about his ability to feel like a man.

Tips for women who want to help their men

1. encourage him to make an appointment with a urologist and offer to go with him. sometimes a man wants to do this on his own and, as his partner, you should honor that.

2. make sure you save time each day to talk with him, and begin talking about exploring new options. the fact that most couples only know how to have sex one or two ways puts more pressure on the man. If he knows there are many ways to please you and if you remain open to new ideas, it will help both of you and your relationship.

3. stress is highly correlated with erectile dysfunction, as is obesity. exercise every day can help alleviate both of these problems. begin a pattern of walking one to two miles together each day. this is also a great way to converse and enjoy each other's company.

Erectile dysfunction is a real condition, but so are aging, stress, conflict, and anxiety. A medication may help relieve the symptoms of ED, but addressing the issues behind the condition may help cure it. Sex is important; it's healthy, and it is good for the marriage. Reassuring your partner that you are a team and will work together is part of the cure.

Understanding Erectile Dysfunction

While more than 52% of American men suffer from some degree of erectile dysfunction, it is surprising how little patients know about the causes and treatments for this disease. Erectile dysfunction can have a significant psychological impact on a man and can significantly impair his relationship with his partner. There are also cultural differences that dictate which men are more likely to seek treatment. For example, Hispanic men are more likely than Asian men to seek treatment.

A questionnaire for men called the Sexual Health Inventory for MALES (SHIM)has been developed to provide a screening questionnaire to help men determine whether they suffer from erectile dysfunction. There are 5 questions with a maximum score of 25. Any score below 19 suggests that a man suffers from erectile dysfunction. (See: http://www.njurology.com/_forms/shim.pdf)

Causes of Erectile Dysfunction

There are many causes of erectile dysfunction. The most common causes are associated with diabetes and prostate cancer. Diabetics are much more likely to have ED because they tend to have poor blood flow and nerve function in the penis. Following prostate cancer surgery many men will develop ED. This can be a devastating consequence for young men or for men who are already very sexually active. Prostate cancer surgery can result in some injury to the nerves that give a man an erection and, unfortunately, some men never regain the ability to have an erection after this surgery. Other causes of ED include smoking, high blood pressure, high cholesterol levels, and certain medications. Many patients don't realize that beta blockers, one of the most commonly used blood pressure medications, can cause problems with erections. Other causes include psychological causes, such as marital guilt, new relationships, and divorce. In these cases sex therapy is extremely effective. Peyronie's disease, which is an abnormal curvature of the penis when it is erect, and penile trauma can also lead to ED.

Sex and the Heart

Erectile dysfunction is important because it is a window to a man's cardiac health and overall physical condition. In fact, the causes of ED and cardiovascular disease are very similar. The common causes include smoking, poor diet and lack of exercise, diabetes, obesity, advanced age, and elevated cholesterol levels. ED is one of the first signs of cardiovascular disease. Studies have shown that from the day a man develops erectile dysfunction, he has a 15% chance of developing a heart attack or stroke within seven years. This means that roughly 1 out of 7 men will have a cardiovascular event if they develop erectile dysfunction! There is a reason for this, and it all has to do with the diameter of a man's arteries. The penile arteries are some of the smallest arteries in a man's body at roughly 1-2mm in diameter. The arteries in the heart are roughly 3-4mm, and the arteries in the neck, or the carotid arteries, 5-6mm. Thus if a man has blockage in his arteries, which arteries do you think are going to get blocked first? The answer is the penile arteries. This is why it is more common for a man to have erectile dysfunction before he has a heart attack and more common for him to have a heart attack before he has a stroke. This is called the "arterial diameter theory," and it makes sense. Thus when a patient comes into my clinic and he has ED and any other risk factors for cardiovascular disease, such as smoking, diabetes, or obesity, I send that patient for a cardiac evaluation because that potentially could save his life. In addition, these men also undergo endothelial testing in my office. The endothelium is the lining of the blood vessels. We use a device that measures how well the blood vessels in the finger dilate. In the mid 2000s, cardiologists showed that, if the blood vessels in the finger do not dilate well, there is good chance that the blood vessels in the heart also will not dilate well and are more likely to be blocked. In the late 2000s, we showed that if the blood vessels in the finger did not dilate well, then patients are more likely to have blocked blood vessels in the penis and suffer from erectile dysfunction. I have seen many men who appeared relatively healthy except for erectile dysfunction and who were found on cardiac evaluation to have blockage of their arteries. Clinicians and patients are becoming increasingly aware that the quality of a man's erections can be the window to the condition of his heart.

The Problem with Viagra

Many people believe that Viagra is a good treatment for erectile dysfunction. One way to take these medications is before sex and the other way is to take a daily dose whether having sex or not. These are referred to as "on-demand" dosing and "daily" dosing, respectively.

The question a man has to ask himself, however, is whether Viagra, or Viagra-like drugs, such as Levitra or Cialis, are really curing the problem of erectile dysfunction. I would argue that these medications are not curing ED but only allowing the disease to become worse over time. The best example I can give is that if you broke your leg to today, you would have two choices. You could treat your leg or you could take pain pills for the rest of your life to mask the pain. If you take the pain pills your leg will only continue to become worse until one day the pain pills are no longer effective and you will not be able to walk. Likewise, with ED, it may also not be possible to fix the problem when long- standing damage has occurred. Using on-demand dosing of these Viagra-like drugs, in my opinion is like taking pain pills for the rest of your life. Many patients do not realize that ED is a disease process that is progressive and that it is actually reversible. Much of what we learned about reversing ED is from the cardiologists. They have shown that they can reverse coronary artery disease by starting patients on a regimented diet and exercise program, prescribing statins (medications used to lower cholesterol), helping them improve their blood pressure and blood sugar levels, and stopping them from smoking. Think about this-- actually reverse heart disease and the plaques in the arteries!

As noted earlier, we now know that heart disease and erectile dysfunction are linked and that they share common causes. It would make sense then that if you could reverse heart disease you should also be able to reverse erectile dysfunction with many of the same treatments that the cardiologists use. This is actually true. Studies have shown that diet and exercise alone can reverse erectile dysfunction. Other studies have shown that the use of statins alone not only improved erectile dysfunction but also made Viagra-like drugs much more effective. Improving diabetic control and stopping smoking are also ways to reverse erectile dysfunction. Finally, daily dosing of Viagra-like drugs, such as Cialis, and the use of testosterone have been shown to reverse erectile dysfunction. Thus

I would much rather treat men with ED with lifestyle modifications, statins, testosterone, and daily Cialis than I would just give them a medication to take before sex. The goal of treatment should be to reverse the disease process or prevent further worsening of the disease.

Respiratory Diseases and Erectile Dysfunction

Chronic obstructive pulmonary disease (COPD) is a common respiratory disease in men. Many people do not realize that shortness and breath and difficulty breathing can lead to erectile dysfunction. The prevalence of erectile dysfunction in patients with respiratory disease has been reported to be as high as 75%. Several studies have shown that worsening of the lung function correlated with the severity of a man's erectile dysfunction.

There are many causes of erectile dysfunction in patients with COPD. The shortness of breath causes decreased oxygen in the brain. This decrease in oxygen affects the erection centers in the brain and inhibits the ability for a man to have an erection. Studies have shown that improvement of lung function or giving oxygen to these patients improves their erections.

Obstructive sleep apnea (OSA) is also a lung problem commonly seen in men, particularly in obese men. OSA is found in up to 10% of men over 40 years of age. Erectile dysfunction has also been found to be associated with OSA, most commonly in the most severe cases of OSA.

Testosterone and Erections

When I entered medical school we were taught that testosterone does NOT improve a man's erections but only improves a man's sex drive. Today we know this is not true. Testosterone is extremely important for a man's overall erectile function. In fact, we now know that drugs used for erections, such as Viagra, Levitra, and Cialis, depend on blood testosterone levels to have their maximum effect. For example, a 62 –year-old man with a low testosterone level complained of failure to respond to Viagra, which had been effective in the past. After he was treated to raise his testosterone levels, the Viagra was effective again. Therefore, I tell other clinicians that if they have a patient not responding to Viagra, Levtira, or Cialis, they should check his testosterone levels because low testosterone could be the problem.

Treatment for Men with Erectile Dysfunction

There are many treatment options for men with ED. The most commonly used medications are the oral medications, such as Viagra, Levitra, Cialis, and the recently introduced Staxyn, which is an oral wafer that dissolves under the tongue. Many men like Staxyn because it can be taken discretely without water. Among other treatments is testosterone therapy, which used alone has been shown to improve erections in men. In addition there are small suppositories (MUSE) that are placed in the tip of the penis where they dissolve and cause blood to enter the penis and cause an erection. Vacuum erection devices, which have been available for many years, are simply cylinders that are placed on the penis to cause a vacuum. This causes an erection and the man then places a band at the base of the penis so that he can maintain his erection. The main benefit of the vacuum is cost. Men have to pay only a one- time cost for the device, and they then do not have to pay every time they have sex. Another very effective treatment for ED is penile injections. These injections place a small amount of fluid at the base of the penis at the 10 and 2 o'clock position. Usually within 5-10 minutes a man is able to achieve a rigid erection sufficient for sex. This is by far the most effective form of therapy and also one of the cheapest if the medication is made at a compounding pharmacy. However, many American men are reluctant to inject their penis with a needle. There is also the penile prosthesis, which was invented in the early 1970s by Dr. Brantley Scott. The penile prosthesis has revolutionized the way we treat men for ED. The penile prosthesis involves a surgical procedure in which an inflatable device is placed in the penis. There is a pump in the scrotum that allows the man to inflate and deflate the prosthesis. The entire prosthesis is placed in the body and is not noticeable if a man takes off his clothes. The benefit of the penile prosthesis is that almost every man can be treated for ED if he is willing to have the procedure. Also a man is able to get an erection whenever he wants for as long as he wants.

Finally, there is sex therapy and counseling.. Every one of Dr. Khera's patients is offered a referral to a sex therapist. Sex therapy is especially helpful for men who suffer from psychological ED. That is, the penis is functioning well enough but there is a mental "block" that prevents them from having erections. These men may wake up with morning erections or have night-time erections, but be unable to achieve erections with their partners. Other examples are men who tell me they are not able to get erections with wives but are able to get good erections with their lovers. These all suggest psychological ED, and counseling with a sex therapist is one of the best forms of therapy.

Treating the Partner

One of the biggest problems I faced when I first started my practice was that many women would call me upset because I had improved their husband's erections. They would tell me that things were great before because the men never asked for sex or pressured them for sex because they were not able to get an erection. Now their improved ability to have an erection was causing marital conflict and stress. The main reason why this was a problem was that the wife did not want to have sex. That's when I started a female sexual dysfunction program. I now treat the wives for sexual dysfunction as well.

Studies have shown that if you increase a woman's sexual desire, her male partner's erections will improve significantly! There are also studies showing that if you improve a man's libido and erections, his wife's libido and sexual function also improve. The reason for this is that **sexual**

dysfunction is a couple's disease. You cannot treat one person without at least addressing the other partner. The best way to treat sexual dysfunction is to treat both partners together.

Other forms of sexual dysfunction in men

Ejaculatory Disorders

Ejaculatory disorders in men include the following: Premature ejaculation, Delayed ejaculation, retrograde ejaculation, Pain or blood with ejaculation, and Low volume ejaculation. These disorders can be caused by a variety of psychological, neurological, hormonal, medical, and surgical conditions. Once other serious related medical problems have been ruled out, a variety of effective behavioral, psychological, medical and surgical treatments are available to patients who suffer from ejaculatory dysfunction.

Premature Ejaculation

Premature ejaculation is the most common sexual disorder in men. It actually is more common than erectile dysfunction and has been reported to occur in as many as 40% of sexually active men. There have been many definitions of premature ejaculation, but the bottom line is that if a man is ejaculating more quickly than he would like, he is suffering from premature ejaculation. While most American men take about 6 minutes to ejaculate, men with premature ejaculation usually ejaculate in less than 1 minute. Interestingly, men from countries in East Asia, such as Japan, China, and Korea, are much more likely to suffer from premature ejaculation than other ethnic groups. Men from the Middle East or African countries are the least likely to suffer from premature ejaculation. Many men do not seek treatment for this problem because they are either too embarrassed or do not believe that treatment exists for this problem. Many of these men avoid sex, and this only strains their relationship with their partners. In fact, the cause of almost all premature ejaculation is mental, and men can be trained to prolong the period before they ejaculate. One of the best treatments for premature ejaculation is sex therapy, which is the only treatment that has been shown to be durable over time.

There are 2 types of premature ejaculation. There is lifelong premature ejaculation, a problem which a man has for his whole life, and there is acquired premature ejaculation, a problem developed later in life. There are many theories about the causes of lifelong premature ejaculation. Many believe that much of premature ejaculation is a learned behavior. When young men initially engage in sexual activity they may learn to ejaculate quickly because they may not have enough time with their partner. As they grow older they bring these learned behaviors with them. Some believe that premature ejaculation is due to anxiety or to an unconscious hostility towards women. Finally, others believe premature ejaculation is due to a problem with the nerves stimulating the penis.

Acquired premature ejaculation is less common and may be due to psychological problems, such as getting a new sexual partner or feeling insecure with a partner. Other causes of acquired premature ejaculation are changes in a man's hormones, such as his thyroid or testosterone, and brain injury such as a stroke. Acquired premature ejaculation could also be due to medications, such as Wellbutrin.

The studies on premature ejaculation are very interesting. We give a couple a stopwatch and we ask them to time their sexual intercourse. The time is called the IELT, or the intravaginal ejaculatory latency time. Before we used the stopwatch technique, we found that many men who had premature ejaculation tended to underestimate their IELT and men who did not have premature ejaculation tended to overestimate their IELT. Therefore the stopwatch method tends to be the most accurate. Also we usually ask the partner to control the stopwatch, as this tends to provide more accurate results.

There are many ways to treat premature ejaculation, but as noted earlier, sex therapy seems to be the most effective and durable over time.

A therapist is able to teach patients techniques that are very effective in prolonging time to ejaculation. There are also many medications that have been used to help men with this premature ejaculation. Unfortunately, most men want to just take a pill rather than to go to therapy, and the most commonly prescribed medications are anti-depressants. Most men do not realize that taking an anti-depressant can significantly delay their ejaculation. While this is good for men who suffer from premature ejaculation, some men find this to be a problem because it takes them too long to ejaculate. Other medications include lidocain gels or sprays that are applied to the penis 5-10 minutes before sex. These gels tend to numb the penis so that a man has decreased pleasure and therefore can last longer. Furthermore, a recent study found that tramadol, a pain medication, prolonged ejaculation in men. In this study, men who had been ejaculating in less than 1 minute were ejaculating after closer to 7 minutes. We do not know how or why this medication works, but I have found it to be effective in my patients. Finally, some studies have shown that Viagra helps treat premature ejaculation. The teaching in sexual medicine is that if a man has both erectile dysfunction and premature ejaculation the erectile dysfunction should be treated first. Remember that the most common type of erectile dysfunction is that related to "venous leak," which prevents a man from maintaining his erection. It's possible that a man is subconsciously aware that he does not have much time to ejaculate before he will lose his erection. In such a case he may develop a pattern of premature ejaculation. Thus, it is not uncommon for men who develop new onset erectile dysfunction to develop premature ejaculation also.

INTERESTING CASE:

A 32-year-old man recently came in to see me because of premature ejaculation. He was very distressed because he was dating several women and this was causing him embarrassment and anxiety. When he came to see me he told me that his problem was erectile dysfunction and did not mention premature ejaculation. After speaking further with him I found that this was not the case. He was referring to the fact that after he had premature ejaculation he was not able to get another erection quickly enough to have sex again immediately. I had to explain to him that not being able to get an erection for some time before having sex again was normal. This is called "refractory time" and tends to be much longer in men than in women. Women can have many orgasms minutes or seconds apart while men usually must wait longer periods before they can have sex again. This patient had developed his own technique for treating premature ejaculation; he would go to the bathroom 1-2 hours before he thought he was going to have sex and he would masturbate. This allowed him to last longer when he actually had sex. He was eventually treated with medications and considers that he no longer has a problem.

What Wives Need To Know About Premature Ejaculation

You probably know at least one, if not several, men who have experienced premature ejaculation. It is one of the most common sexual problems men struggle with, but no one talks about it. When couples seek help both partners often are equally frustrated. The saddest part of PE is that so many isolate themselves and keep quiet rather than risk feelings of inadequacy when talking to their health care professional. Many men who aren't married quit dating because of embarrassment and frustration. The partner of someone who has PE can help significantly if she knows what to do.

Premature ejaculation has many components, and each man is unique. There are biological causes, psychological causes, medication causes, and behavioral causes. From an evolutionary perspective, sex should be quick. Sex is for procreation; the faster you are, the greater the chance of reproducing. Although enjoyable sex is not meant to be fast, evolutionary theorists would hold to the theory that men are programmed that way.

When sex lasts one to three minutes or less (which is typical for men with PE) no one enjoys sex, including the man. Treatment for premature ejaculation should always begin with a visit to a physician. Usually a family doctor will refer you to a Urologist, who specializes in sexual dysfunction. There are medications that can be used to help prolong an erection or reduce anxiety; many times this visit is all you will need. When PE has been consistent over several years in a marriage or relationship, there is usually emotional damage that must be dealt with between the partners. People say unkind things to each other when sex is frustrating, and many couples quit trying to have sex. This can be hurtful to the both partners and create resentment and anger in the marriage.

Guidelines For Approaching Treatment For Premature Ejaculation.

1. The first thing you must do is sit down with your partner and talk about it. Tell your partner how it makes you feel. Do this at a time when you are both relaxed and not frustrated. Tell your partner some of the reasons you believe you struggle with it. As the partner, be sure to listen openly and without judgment. Remember the goal is for both of you to be able to express yourselves in a healthy loving way.

2. Learning about your own body and being aware of the feeling right before ejaculation is very important. Therefore, masturbation is very important. When you masturbate make sure you do it by yourself with no distraction. Instead of going quickly, slow down so you can become more aware of your physical reactions.

3. Sex is more than penetration. As a couple it is important that you explore all areas of each other's bodies. Touching, smelling, and kissing are all wonderful ways to share a sexual connection as well as please one another. When you have more options, you reduce the anxiety about the need to perform. Sex toys provide options, as do massage oils and powders.

4. Yoga is a wonderful activity for men who suffer from pe. It helps men learn how their breathing is affecting their pe; it teaches them to slow down and control their breathing. It also offers exercises to help strengthen and stretch the pelvic floor muscles. Yoga benefits most sexual responses in both men and women.

attending a yoga class for couples would be a wonderful option in treating pe.

5. Consider counseling as a couple. many times when men have pe, They believe it is their fault and their responsibility to fix. When you are a couple, you learn very quickly that what affects one partner affects both. for better or worse, this is one problem that is handled better as a couple than an individual. Counseling can help open the communication between partners, which often is 90% of the problem.

Premature ejaculation can wreak havoc on a relationship. However, it can also be a catalyst for creating a closer and more intimate relationship. Sharing a common problem many times helps bond the couple. The key is viewing the problem as something both partners work at solving rather than considering it "his" problem. The brain is the largest sex organ; PE has a lot to do with how a man feels about his ability to please his partner. *Delayed Orgasm Or Absent Orgasm.*

While most men are concerned about premature ejaculation, some men have the opposite problem. These men take too long to ejaculate and at times they cannot ejaculate or have an orgasm at all. This can build frustration not only for the man but also for his partner. Remember that most of an orgasm is mental. Some men tell me that they may have this problem with their wives, but not their mistresses or other sexual partners. This suggests that there is a psychological element that is inhibiting these men from reaching orgasm. Other causes of delayed orgasm or inability to have an orgasm are medications, stress, fatigue, and certain drugs. Alcohol and marijuana are commonly known to delay orgasm. Anti-depressants and psychiatric drugs are also very commonly seen to impair orgasm. As noted earlier, antidepressants are sometimes used to treat premature ejaculation.

Stress can come in many forms, personal, work-related, and physical. Many times men are stressed about a situation but do not realize that it is causing them to have sexual problems. For example, a 74-year-old patient suddenly developed an inability to have an orgasm. He and his wife had traditionally been very sexually active and they both were very distressed about this problem. Conversation with this patient revealed that his brother was dying in a hospice and this was really upsetting him. After he was able to understand what was subconsciously bothering him and after sex therapy treatment, he was able to have normal orgasms again. Many times patients just need to work through the mental block they are creating when they engage in sex.

While sex therapy is an excellent way to treat delayed orgasm or absent orgasm, there are many medications that are used off-label that may help. Dopamine is a chemical in the brain that helps increase the ability to have an orgasm. Therefore, we use medications that increase dopamine in the brain and this, many times, is very effective. Certain medications used to improve orgasm include Wellbutrin, dostinex, and yohimbine. All of these medications, if used, should be prescribed only by a physician, and patients should be monitored closely.

Retrograde (Backward) Ejaculation

When a man ejaculates, the sperm travel from the testicles to the prostate. At this point the semen has an option to go backwards into the bladder or forward and out through the penis. Fortunately men have a bladder neck, or valve, which closes during ejaculation and does not allow the semen to go into the bladder. The closure of this valve forces the semen to go out through the penis. There are times when the valve does not work properly and the semen goes into the bladder. Many men are very concerned because they have the pleasure of the orgasm, but do not see anything come out of their penis. The causes of retrograde ejaculation include taking certain medications, such as those for an enlarged prostate, surgeries on the bladder or prostate, or having a certain medical condition such as diabetes. Sometimes the retrograde ejaculation is only partial, and men with this problem complain of a significant decline in their semen volume.

Blood in the Ejaculate

Blood in the ejaculate can be very distressing for most men and their partners. Most of the time this is not serious and will resolve on its own. The bleeding usually is due to infection or inflammation. If the bleeding in the ejaculate does not resolve, a man should be evaluated by a Urologist. In older men particularly, blood in the ejaculate rarely may be a sign of prostate cancer.

Pain with Ejaculation

Pain with ejaculation can have many causes and can be located in many areas, such as in the testicles, in the lower abdomen, or underneath the scrotum. Men may try to avoid sex because they are fearful that they are hurting their bodies or making the condition worse. Often this pain is due to an infection or inflammation, which usually resolves. Sometimes the pain is due to a blockage of the tubes coming from the testicle to the penis. The blockage could be the result of a previous vasectomy or due to cysts that form over time in the prostate. The blockage can also lead to a significant decline in the amount of fluid that comes out with each ejaculation. There are tests that can be done in the office to see if a patient does have blockage of these tubes. The good news is that these tubes can be opened surgically.

Low Volume Ejaculation

I am surprised that so many men become concerned when they notice a decline in the volume of their ejaculate. These men come in seeking ways to increase the amount of ejaculate. A low ejaculatory volume could have many causes, including a low testosterone level, retrograde ejaculation, or blockage of the tubes carrying the semen. However, it is also true that production of less semen is a natural part of aging.

Peyronie's Disease

Up to 9% of men experience an abnormal curvature of their penis when it is erect. This is known as Peyronie's disease. The most common cause of Peyronie's disease is penile trauma that occurs during sexual intercourse. The penis develops a scar, and this scar can then cause the penis to bend when it is erect. Significant penile curvatures can result in pain, poor erections, and an inability to engage in sexual intercourse. When the penis bends more than 60 degrees, this is generally prohibitive for sex. Many men are extremely distressed by this curvature of their penis. Studies have found that some men equate the severity of getting Peyronie's disease to a death in the family. There are many support groups available to help these patients. A useful website for more information is www.peyroniesassociation.org.

Traditionally, treatments for this problem have been limited, and they often are unsuccessful. However, new medical therapies that prevent the scar formation and promote scar breakdown can be effective in up to 70 percent of patients. Some men may require penile injections with medication to reduce the plaque size and prevent progression of plaque. Other therapies include penile stretching devices. Surgical correction and penile straightening procedures are available to men who do not respond to more conservative medical treatments.

SEXUAL DYSFUNCTION IN WOMEN

Understanding the Anatomy

When a woman is stimulated sexually, many changes occur in her body. First there is increased blood flow to her breasts and genitalia. The walls of the vagina become engorged and they thicken. The walls then start to release fluid into the vagina. The vagina starts to expand backwards to accommodate or make room for the penis. At the same time the clitoris becomes full and congested. The increased blood flow in the breasts results in erection of the nipples. The rest of the body is also undergoing significant changes at this time. Muscle tension throughout the body is increased, and heart rate and blood pressure may increase slightly.

The next phase, called the "plateau" phase, is the phase just before a woman reaches orgasm. She has reached her maximum point of excitement and the physiologic changes described above become intensified and her labia are enlarged. It has been suggested that orgasm does not occur until labial congestion reaches its peak. The clitoris retracts and almost disappears from view. Changes in the vagina cause lengthening, and its outer third becomes more congested and narrow. Skin flush spreads, and there are further increases in muscle tension, blood pressure, and heart rate

The "orgasmic" phase is a peak of physiologic and psychological pleasure. An orgasm in a woman is really focused on the outer 1/3 of her vagina. If you think of the vagina as a tube the inner 2/3 is deeper in her body and closer to her uterus. During orgasm, the outer 1/3 of the vagina contracts rapidly and rhythmically many times. In fact studies have shown that the outer 1/3 of the vagina contracts more than once every second. The uterus also contracts, with movement starting at the top and working its way down to the cervix and vagina. Other changes include increases in blood pressure, respiration, heart rate, pelvic thrusts, and involuntary contraction of the rectal sphincter.

The final stage is called the "resolution" phase. There is a slow disappearance of vaginal and breast engorgement and swelling and a return to normal size.

The Biology of the Female Sexual Response

The female sexual response is a dynamic process influenced by biological, psychological and sociocultural factors. One of the first descriptions of this response was published by Masters and Johnson in the 1960s when they described the linear response. In this model they described a linear 4-phase model of sexual response: excitement, plateau, orgasm, and resolution. The problem with this model is that it assumes that a woman has to have desire before arousal, and this is not necessarily true. A woman can be aroused before she has the desire to have sex.

Later, in 2001, Basson described a circular model for the female sexual response. (Figure 1) This model incorporates the importance of emotional intimacy, sexual stimuli, and biologic and psychosocial issues, such as self image or a history of sexual abuse. In this model, sexual desire is not needed before engaging in sex, but it helps. For example, a woman's desire for emotional intimacy can allow her to be receptive to sexual stimuli and thus engage in sex. Or in other cases, women can be aroused without any sexual stimuli and can start from here in the cycle. Eventually this leads to desire, emotion, and physical satisfaction, and then, depending on how emotionally and physically satisfying the experience is, can drive the cycle again.

According to Basson, women have many reasons for engaging in sexual activity other than sexual hunger or drive. Many midlife women in long-term relationships do not have a great deal of spontaneous desire and interest, but engage in sex due to a desire for increased emotional intimacy with their partners. They start from a position of sexual neutrality, where they are responsive to engaging in sexual activity if their partners approach them but don't initiate sexual activity. Once aroused, sexual desire emerges and motivates them to continue the activity. This model clarifies how vulnerable a woman's sexual response is and that the goal of sexual activity for women is not necessarily orgasm, but rather personal satisfaction.

Are Women Having Sex?

In a survey in 2003, 2000 US women were randomly dialed by phone to assess their sexual practices and health behaviors. Questions about sexual practices and health behaviors during a typical 4-week period were included in the questionnaire, as were questions about medical history, vaginal symptoms, and sociodemographic variables. "Sexually active" was defined as having oral (active or receptive), vaginal, or anal intercourse in the past 3 months.

The percentage of sexually active women per age group is shown in Figure 3.

According to this study, it is not true that of the women between the ages of 18 and 49, the younger women tended to have more sex. In fact, the percentage of sexually active women is fairly consistent across this age group. A noticeable drop in sexual encounters occurs in the women in their 50s. One of the main reasons is that women go through menopause at roughly 51 years of age, and they experience a precipitous decline in their hormones. Another reason for the decline is that this is the time when many men start to develop erectile dysfunction.

What is more surprising is that women who are not having sex, but who are concerned about their decreased sexual desire, are not seeking formal treatment for their problem. A recent study found that only 35% of women got help from a health care provider. The study showed that of the women with distressing sexual problems, 42% sought help from informal sources, defined as someone other than a health care provider; 35% sought help from a formal source, such as a health care provider; 9% sought help from an anonymous source such as the Internet, television, radio, or printed material, and 15% did not seek help

Defining Female Sexual Dysfunction

Approximately 43% of women suffer from some degree of female sexual dysfunction, or FSD. This is a major problem within our society; yet there is still little awareness of it, and few treatment options are available. There are 4 main categories for FSD. These include disorders of sexual desire, arousal disorders, orgasmic disorders, and pain with intercourse. Disorders of sexual desire are the most common. Many factors, such as her overall health, hormone status, fatigue, self-image, stress, and the quality of her relationship can decrease a women's desire for sex. Arousal disorders affect up to 31 percent of women with FSD. These women may have the desire to have sex, but do not experience sexual arousal, which includes increased blood flow to the breast and genitalia and increased vaginal lubrication before and during sex. Female orgasmic disorder can be defined as delay in or inability to have an orgasm following sufficient sexual stimulation and arousal which causes personal distress. Some women may also experience "situational" orgasmic disorders in which they can only have an orgasm in certain situations, such as on vacation or with a lover. Pain disorders are also common, especially in postmenopausal women when they lose their vaginal estrogen. Some other common causes of pain disorders, such as vulvar vestibulitis, are more difficult to treat and many require surgical intervention.

The medical condition of low libido in women has been renamed Hypoactive Sexual Desire Disorder, or HSDD. This is a medical condition which causes women to suffer from a lack of desire to engage in sexual activity. A simple questionnaire has recently been developed for HSDD called the Decreased Sexual Desire Screener, or DSDS. (See http://www.omniaeducation.com/whav/WHAV_Addenda2/Decreased_Sexual_Desire_Screener_DSDS_Female_Sexual_Dysfunction_Tool.pdf) DSDS was specifically developed for use by clinicians not necessarily trained in FSD to identity women suffering from HSDD. If a patient answers "NO" to any of questions 1 through 4 the diagnosis of acquired HSDD does not apply. If a patient answers "YES" to all questions 1 through 4 and clinicians verified "NO" to all factors in question 5 the patient has generalized, acquired HSDD. If the patient answers "YES" to all questions 1 through 4 and "YES" to any of the factors in question 5, the clinician must use his/her best judgment to determine the diagnosis.

A female sexual dysfunction (FSD) evaluation consists of a detailed history and physical examination. This also involves completing pre-clinic questionnaires for the patient and her partner. The most commonly used questionnaire for women is referred to as the Female Sexual Function Index, or the FSFI. (http://www.obgynalliance.com/files/fsd/FSFI_Pocketcard.pd) Most women will have laboratory testing to evaluate hormone levels as well as to look for other causes of FSD, such as hypothyroidism. If indicated, some women will have specialized testing such as genital ultrasound, quantitative sensory testing, or endothelial function testing.

Treating Female Sexual Dysfunction

An algorithm (action plan) is used for treating FSD which involves identification, education, modification, medical therapy, and surgery (if needed).

- Treatment primarily involves **identification** of the problem, such as a desire disorders or pain disorders. Identification of the problem is made through the history, physical examination, questionnaire responses, and laboratory and specialized testing.
- After the problem is identified, we focus on **educating** the patient and her partner about female sexual dysfunction, the female anatomy, and the causes and treatments for the different types of sexual dysfunction disorders.
- • Many times **modifications** will have to be made in a woman's lifestyle
- (i.e. diet, exercise, stress reduction) or in her medications. Women may need to undergo biofeedback or relaxation techniques.
- **Medical therapy** involves hormonal and non-hormonal treatments. Hormonal treatments many include estrogen and/or testosterone replacement therapy. Non-hormonal treatments include medications such as Wellbutrin or certain natural herbs.
- **Surgical therapy** is indicated in only a select group of women, particularly those who suffer from pain disorders. Surgical procedures include labioplasty, vestibulectomy, and incontinence procedures.

All women receive a referral to see a sex therapist. The treatment of FSD is much more challenging than treating men for ED and really requires focus on all aspects of a woman's life. It is said that "women have to reduce their stress to have sex and men have sex to reduce their stress". This tends to be true and further illustrates the differences in treating men and women for sexual dysfunction.

Emotional Health

Sexual health is emotional as well as physical and is treated with counseling as well as medicine. No matter what physical and medical problems Bob and Lilly solve, they will also have to deal with emotional issues in order to regain their closeness s a couple. Body image and obesity play important roles in sexual function in both women and men.

Body Image in Women : Body image is highly correlated with sexuality. In the *Journal of Sex Research* Dr. Patricia Barthalow Koch recently reported a study showing that negative body image was one of the top reasons women report for not wanting to have sex. Men may have difficulty understanding this because many of them tell their wives every day how beautiful they are only to find that their wives still don't want to have sex. Husbands may not understand that their wives don't derive their body image from what their husbands say. Their complements may be helpful and reassuring, but what is crucial is that she believe that she is beautiful and desirable. **In other words, if she beats herself up, or is critical of her looks when she compares herself to others, his flattery falls on deaf ears, no matter what he says.**

The one thing both women and men agree turns them on is how a woman looks. The problem is that women's ideas of what makes them beautiful or sexy are so different from men's, and all are so varied that it is difficult to arrive at a consistent definition. What we do know is that when women take time for themselves they feel sexier, better about their bodies, and more willing to share their bodies with their partners.

Sexuality and body hate

It has been reported that the three most likely disincentives to sex for married women are fatigue, boredom, and, most prevalent, a negative body image. Women worried about whether their partner was looking at their cellulite, seeing their fat roll, or fantasizing about larger breasts than they actually had.

A popular woman's magazine recently reported results of a survey in which more than 300 women of all shapes and sizes reported on what they say to themselves each day. They averaged 13 negative thoughts about their bodies each day. That wasn't all; many reported more than 100 each day. Can you imagine what you would feel like if you told yourself all day each hour how ugly, fat, stupid, or skinny you are? Dr. Anne Kearney-Cooke (Cincinnati Psychotherapy Institute), who has done expansive research in this area, says the results of the survey are not surprising. More and more we are conditioning young girls to worry about how they look, to compare themselves to friends, and to look like the celebrities they see on TV and read about in teen magazines. If women now in their 30s, 40's, and 50's feel the pressure of not looking good enough, or being valued for their beautiful curves and body shape, can you imagine what the next generation will feel like? Face Book, MTV, Reality TV, as well as most magazines, tell girls and women what they are supposed to look like. There is a correlation between how we feel about our bodies at the age of 9 and 10 and how we feel when we are adults. That correlation is going to influence whether or not women can enjoy having someone love them, and be sexually healthy as adults.

The International Society for the Study of Women's Sexual Health has begun a major push to study women because most of what we believe is true with women's sexuality was based on what is true for men. We are finding that the sexes are very different in their experience of sex. Women have many excuses not to engage in sex; many of these excuses have nothing to do with their partners. Their rejection is mostly of themselves. Medications and counseling may help some women deal with their depression or anxiety about negative body image, but these methods may not cure or prevent these feelings. We need to begin thinking about what we are telling women about their bodies. And women need to start questioning the source of the image they are using as their models.

The easiest way to begin is to set aside time each week to work on improving your body image. People who feel good about themselves are happier, and more successful at work and in their relationships.

Tips for improving body image

- for everything you say critically about your body, tell yourself one good thing. for example if you are talking about your "roll around the middle" make note out loud about your beautiful eyes or smile.
- your body hears everything you say. I don't know how it happens, but people who continue to berate themselves actually seem to exaggerate the flaw they berate. I have watched and listened as obese patients who talk about how "fat" they are continued to gain weight. the body reacts to what you tell it.
- movement and body awareness are important. touch your body; understand it. exercise helps women feel much more capable and confident. You don't have to run a marathon, but you do need to feel the euphoria of a brisk walk or swim.
- What you don't like about your body might be a reflection of something more complicated. If you are at a party and want to impress a particular person, you may all of a sudden become very self-conscious about your nose. your nose didn't change at the party; it is your insecurity in yourself. try to address the real issue. being afraid of rejection is different from hating your nose.
- men often are not the problem, ladies. **We have to own our sexuality and accept our bodies before we can be comfortable with our man and happy with ourselves.**

Body Image in Men : The Short Penis. Many men are fixated on penile size. Clearly, if his penis is not long enough to penetrate his partner a man may experience psychological distress. However, most men are able to penetrate their partners but just have the impression that their penis is too short. They tend to believe that the longer the penis, the better, and the more pleasure they are able to give to their partners. This is not true. The "G" spot is located just under the clitoris in women, and this is where women receive much of their pleasure during sex. Thus the wider the penis, the more stimulation the G spot should experience. If a man can penetrate his partner and keep his penis penetrated during sex, the wider the penis the better. Therefore, men should think more about width and not so much about length.

There are several reasons why a man might develop a short penis. The first is age. As men get older, their muscles shrink. We call this atrophy. Remember that the penis is a muscle, and this muscle needs to expand in order for a man to get an erection. Other reasons for developing a short penis are Peyronie's disease, which is an abnormal curvature of the penis when it is erect, and prostate cancer surgery. Men also complain of loss of penile size when they have trauma to their penis or surgery on their penis. Obese men develop a condition called "buried penis" which occurs when the fat above the penis causes the penis to be pulled back in. Losing weight in this case can help tremendously in regaining penile length and size.

One of the best treatments for increasing penile length is the use of penile stretching devices. These devices are worn 2-6 hours per day and can be concealed under a man's clothes. The penis is placed through this device and a securing tape is placed just behind the head of the penis. The device is spring loaded, and men are advised to increase the length of the springs every 2-3 weeks. Several studies have shown a significant increase not only in penile length, but also in penile width after use of these devices for 6 months. The stretchers are not covered by most insurance companies but cost around $300. If a man cannot afford a penile stretching device and also has erectile dysfunction, a physician may prescribe a vacuum erection device which also will allow him to stretch his penis. A vacuum erection device is a cylindrical tube into which the penis is placed; suction is established and an erection is achieved. These devices are affordable and many are covered by insurance. In Dr. Khera's opinion, stretching techniques for the penis seem to be the safest and most reliable ways to increase penile length and width.

INTERESTING CASE:

Last year I had a patient who had gone to Florida to have a bulking agent injected under his penile skin to make his penis larger and wider. Many bulking agents, such as collagen, are being used for this purpose. However, I strongly discourage this action. In this case the penis started to undergo necrosis, or started dying. It turned black, and eventually I had to remove his penis. He later went on to have a new penis made from his forearm muscle, but as you can imagine, it is not quite the same. While penile length may be important to most men, some men are obsessed with this concept and will do almost anything to increase the length of their penis. I urge caution with surgeries and cosmetic procedures to increase penile length as the complications can be devastating. Dealing with real or perceived penile inadequacy

Just as women focus on their faces and overall looks, men focus on penis size and appearance. .Men who believe that they don't measure up or that their penis is not attractive may suffer from low self-esteem and loss of confidence. They may be reluctant to date, and find themselves unable to establish relationships. When a man thinks that his penis is inadequate in size or appearance, talking to him about it seems impossible. He feels regret and shame about it, and even if those who love him most aren't complaining, it makes no difference. If he has a partner, there are exercises the couple can do that will enhance communication and help reassure him.

For men with a small penis there are simple things to be done that will make him feel better about the appearance of his penis. Men who are overweight many times begin to feel better when they lose weight. Enrolling in a fitness program and being encouraged to lose weight as well as working out can make them feel more masculine as well as help the penis appear larger. Another thing a man can do is shave around the base of his penis. This allows the penis to look larger and may be more atheistically appealing to the man and his partner. It also may heighten sensitivity and may be more pleasing for oral sex.

The problem is that a man's overall feelings about his penis won't improve until he is able to alter the size, accept the size, or focus on being a skilled lover. That is why it is common for patients to be seeing both a physician and a counselor at the same time.

The psychological loss with Peyronie's Disease

Peyronie's disease may be disfiguring, depending on the intensity of plaque, and may cause feelings of shame and embarrassment due to the appearance of the penis. This can lead to social isolation and affect a man's ability to seek help. His Peyronie's may leave him unable to make love, or feel sufficiently confident to establish a relationship. Depression is common, and because of their isolation, many of these men don't bother with treatment for the depression or anxiety either. When men experience depression, it is not uncommon for them to ask "Why me?" "Who would be able to love me like this?" or to act out with anger and blame. Men are fixers, and this problem has many dimensions to fix.

- The main key for men is to fight the urge to withdraw or become isolated because that will only serve to make the feeling more intense, the anger greater, and the ability to work with a partner impossible.
- When men are single or unattached, joining a Peyronie's support group is mandatory. These groups have a very strong healing component because when you have Peyronie's you tend to think you are the only person in the world with it. When other men are talking about their disease, it provides a "comfort level" that allows a man to be honest and own up to his feelings. He becomes braver, and begins seeing himself as part of the solution rather than a victim to the problem.

- Peyronie's is a couple's disease, so men who work with their partners to deal with their disease have an easier time taking back their sexuality and their ability to express themselves. The partners will be better able to rediscover and improve their love making if they are open to trying new things and positions. Their reassurance will make a huge difference to the person suffering from Peyronie's. The best way to deal with Peyronie's is to find a Urologist and a counselor you can work with as a couple. As with any disease, stress exacerbates the issue, so learning new ways of coping with the ordinary stressors of life will help lessen the impact Peyronie's has in a relationship.

Sexual Function and Obesity

Obesity can have a significant effect not only on body image but also on overall normal sexual function. One study looking at women found that the greater a woman's weight or body mass index (BMI), the less likely she was to be able to experience sexual arousal, orgasm, and overall sexual satisfaction. Another study found that obese men were twice as likely to suffer from erectile dysfunction (ED) as non-obese men.

There are several reasons why obesity can hurt overall sexual function in both men and women. One reason is that obese patients are more likely to have a decline in their blood testosterone levels. Obese patients not only produce less testosterone, but also convert more of their testosterone to estrogen. As noted earlier testosterone is responsible for sexual drive in both men and women.

Obese patients tend to have a poor self-body image and this can lead to psychological ED for which sex therapy is extremely helpful. Obese patients also tend to have other co-morbid conditions, such as diabetes and hypertension. These co-morbid conditions are strong risk factors for erectile dysfunction. Finally some male patients do not have penile length sufficient for penetration because the fat above the penis tends to pull a ligament attached to the penis which draws it back into the body.

Many investigators have studied obesity and sex, and they have reported some interesting findings. For instance, it has been reported that there is a significant correlation between the size of someone's waist and the number of times they have sex? The larger a person's waist the less likely they are to have sex. In fact, other studies have shown that the larger a man or woman's waist the more likely they are to masturbate. This may be due to the fact that they are insecure about their body image or that they are not able to find a partner as easily as thinner people. An interesting observation is that obese patients tend to become hypersexual after they lose weight, such as after bariatric surgery. This could be due to improved self-body image, improved overall health, an increase in their testosterone levels, or their ability to overcome positional issues. A recent study found that 11% of obese women did not engage in sexual activity because of their body size.

INTERESTING CASE

One problem I see is that patients who undergo obesity surgery tend to become hypersexual after surgery, and this can cause problems for their partner. A couple recently came to see me after the wife underwent bariatric surgery. She had become hypersexual and this had caused problems with their marriage as the husband was not as interested in having sex. He had mentioned to me that had he known she was going to be this sexual after her surgery he never would have tried to convince her to have the surgery. He was concerned that if he did not have sex with her she would have an affair and have sex with someone else. The key to this problem was treating him for sexual dysfunction. He was also obese, had a low testosterone level, and a poor self-body image. I prescribed testosterone replacement therapy, a diet and exercise program, and sent him for sex therapy. These had a significant impact on his desire for sex and the quality of his erections. He told me that he believed this saved his marriage. Thus it is important to treat not only the patient but the partner as well. The treatment for sexual dysfunction should focus not on the individual, but on the couple.

Losing weight

We have learned that obesity alone can cause poor body image and reduced self-esteem. Diabetes that frequently accompanies obesity causes problems with blood flow. For men it affects maintaining as well as achieving an erection, and for women it causes difficulty with lubrication. No one wants to have sex when they are in pain and many times obese patients suffer hip, back, or other joint pain. Encouraging patients to follow a healthy life style plan is never as effective as commitment by the couple to work together to restore a healthy body weight and a healthy sex life. There are things couples can do to help maintain a healthy lifestyle and lose weight.

Before they begin a program, it is helpful if they understand a few basics about men's and women's bodies in relationship to losing weight:

- Men lose faster. They have more muscle mass, faster metabolism, and more water. Therefore, the same exercise and diet will be reflected differently on the scales. Women lose more slowly, and the body fluctuates more due to menstruation and higher fat content.

- Women get hungrier than men with strenuous exercise. Women's bodies are designed to give birth, so they feel the need to restore what they burn.

- Both men and women can be addicted to trigger foods, but it is more common with women. If your partner understands this, you can ban specific foods from your home.

Tips for a successful program of exercise and diet as a couple

- Choose an exercise you both want to do. It should be carried out at a level that allows you to continue to talk to each other, thus enhancing your emotional connection, as well as improving your cardiovascular health.

- Choose the number of times each week you will engage in this activity and the time. If you are a morning person and your partner is an evening person, maybe you can go together on the weekends and separately during the week.

- don't compare your weight loss with your partner's. What is important is that you encourage each other. Congratulate each other on appearance and clothing size as you lose weight. Is your partner more energetic? happier? these are the things to notice.

- take turns cooking healthy food. make dinners at home special. this will save money as well as reduce unwanted calories.

- If you feel a binge coming on, alert your partner that you need additional support to stay on track. many times just telling someone else will stop the binge before it starts.

- supervise yourself only. don't become the sergeant to your spouse. the goal is to get healthier and whittle away the waist, not your marriage.

- prepare for more intimacy. Women, especially. are more desirous of sex when they feel better about their bodies. sometimes losing one or two inches from her waist can turn a woman into a sex goddess.

- be consistent. It takes about 30 days to make a behavior a habit. everyone has the money and means to live a healthier lifestyle.

- With weight loss, as with everything else, you get better results when you encourage rather than shame.

- the more couples engage in activities together, the happier they report their marriage. the more couples share a vision, the happier they report being. losing weight with your partner achieves both of these.

a few more tips
- **reward yourself**: every time one of you hits a goal, reward yourselves together. the reward must not be something to eat..

- **Split restaurant meals**: Whenever you dine together, cut your calories in half by splitting meals.

- **make sure sex is part of your exercise.** sex burns calories and reinforces the team spirit.

- **don't make dining a date**: make your date nights "movement nights". take a walk, golf, bowl, or shoot pool.

- **Focus on health not weight.** If you focus on getting healthier you can embrace your life style with more determination than if you focus on being able to fit into a particular suit or dress.

Both men and women have better sex when they are able to communicate their feelings with regard to being in their bodies. If one partner doesn't like his or her body, open communication can help both partners understand what specifically is the problem. Many times a negative body image linked to feeling fat or having small breasts or a small penis is really the result of much more than concerns about a specific body part. When patients have engaged in weight loss surgery, breast augmentation or penile enlargement they may continue to have depression and low self-esteem. The negative body image may have much more to do with what others who were powerful in your life may have said about your body. It's almost as if they planted "tapes" in your head that continue to play without your permission. Medication may help with the thoughts being played over and over, but only counseling can help re-write the tapes or manage them. And, of course, having a partner with you who loves you and can help in the treatment process is much more effective than trying to overcome these feelings on your own.

In summary: **Fix what you can, and learn to love what's left.**

STEP 3 GET SET: RE-ESTABLISH INTIMACY AND RE-ENERGIZE CONTACT

Up Close and Intimate

Lilly and Robert arrive for their appointment looking fit and happy. Dr. Khera, working with Lilly's gynecologist, has made a change in Lilly's birth control pills and is working with Robert to find the best treatment for his ED. They still seem awkward around each other. They have improved the pattern of their daily lives and addressed their psychological and health issues, but haven't achieved the intimacy that will make them into a "couple" again.

Sometimes lack of desire has a physical cause that can be treated medically or an emotional cause that can be addressed with a counselor, but sometimes, even when these problems have been addressed, couples are unable to enjoy a satisfactory sex life.

- **Relationship issues.** Anger, resentment, guilt, shame, and jealousy are some of the underlying issues that cause decreased desire for sex in a relationship. Below is a letter from a woman seeking sex counseling? You can read between the lines that her husband feels resentment due to her lack of sexual interest. The first issue I will address with her is not his resentment, but the importance of her reclaiming her sex life, not only to keep her husband at home, but also to improve her overall health.

Dear Mary Jo,

I am 50 years old and have been married for 23 years, and my lack of initiating sex has driven our relationship to the breaking point. My husband is very frustrated sexually and says he feels trapped. We were discussing how

I am not turned on by the sight of his penis, and my lack of interest in oral sex. I would like to set up some counseling with you as I would like to have a strong sexual relationship with my husband. We get along in most other areas, but this area could drive him to another woman, and I don't want that!

What you can do? Sit down with your partner and discuss how you are feeling. Many couples do not deal with their emotional issues, expecting sex to heal the relationship. Healthy sex happens when the couple feels close and intimate. Resentment or feeling unloved builds a wall that dampens libido. If there are issues that you cannot work through and your physician has advised you that your sex drive is not related to physical reasons, then it is time to find a counselor. Working with a counselor can help you unravel the emotions that are preventing you from feeling passion with your partner.

Some investigators have described a tipping point theory. A woman will weigh all the negative and positive factors of the biospsychosocial model and if the net result is positive, she will engage in sexual activity. This is very different from men who do not tend to put as much emphasis on these different factors.

The time has come to work on intimacy and romance.

A lack of sex can't kill a relationship, but a lack of intimacy may. Being held close and feeling loved and desired is important to all of us.

Sex is important, but a relationship cannot thrive on sex alone. On many levels women and men do not understand each other. It is not rare in my practice for men to come in telling me they have a great marriage, but miss the intimacy with their spouse. Wives, on the other hand, may feel that they are not good enough. They aren't worrying about intimacy but fearing that if they aren't having sex often enough, their husbands may stray. This usually is not the case. In fact, most men love their wives dearly and they would do anything to keep them happy. They are proud of their wives' ability to raise healthy children, and they brag about their wives' attractiveness, cooking, and passion for life. Women many times don't know this; I am not sure whether it is a lack of communication or time, but husbands are not always good at communicating their appreciation.

Many women believe that what their husbands want most is sex. This is true to some degree, but men want more than sex—they want the connection with their wives. They use this connection to feel close to her when they travel or are away from her. This need for intimacy increases as men get older. When a man is 40-years-old he may want to feel more emotionally connected than he did at 30 years of age. As women get older they may feel more stress, and they forget that it is lack of intimacy, and not sex, that can kill their marriage. They may have sex, but they may not put their heart or feelings into it. They may have candle-lit dinners with their husbands, but have nothing to say. Intimacy helps create the "vision" for the marriage. Intimacy offers a common goal that will inspire the marriage. Intimacy provides the opportunity to talk about making the marriage better and actually having new ideas about how to grow closer to each other. (Complaining about a lack of sex or some other problem is not a way to build intimacy). Increased sex can help build intimacy, but it is NOT intimacy. Without intimacy the couple loses the desire to have sex.

Are you bored?

No matter how attractive you are to each other when you get married and no matter how long you are married before it begins, you may have to deal with boring sex at some point. **Boring sex happens briefly in many marriages.** In other marriages, boring sex can become the only type of sex. It is easy to understand how this can come about. You share your life, your bed, and your being with another person that you know and love. The most intimate thing a couple shares is their love making. If couples get *too busy* to communicate and experiment with their expressions of love, then sex begins to feel routine and unconnected.

Many things can cause boredom in the bedroom—some of them discussed already --waning hormones, body image, marital conflict, not knowing one's body, or having a lover who doesn't know how to make love. About one third of all the couples who seek counseling indicate that "boredom" is the underlying problem in their marriage. Boredom doesn't always present itself as boredom, however. Few couples will come in and say, "We are bored with each other." Boredom disguises itself in other problems such as, "She doesn't want to have sex with me anymore," or, "He/she cheated on me." Couples rarely sit down and say to each other, "My sex life is boring me, how do you feel?" Since they aren't comfortable discussing their feelings with their partners, they open themselves to finding another lover or they completely withdraw from having sex.

You can become closer to your partner by discussing your feelings and working together to make your sex life breathe again. Trying to fix it by reaching out to another person won't make your sex life with your husband or wife better. In the long run, you will be dealing with boredom again in a new bed.

Things to do to make a boring bedroom exciting again.

1. Talk about the problem. to talk about this problem identify it from the perspective of both partners.
2. Be gentle. telling a partner he or she doesn't turn you on usually means you have not been transparent about what does turn you on.
3. Go to a sex store or shop online. buying powders or lotions is a wonderful way to start. It helps make sex fun, and sex that is fun is not boring.
4. Try making love in different rooms, and forget the idea that you need to make love in a bed. Women are more sensitive to location changes than men. If your lady tells you she is bored with sex, try changing up where you make love.
5. Visiting a urologist who specializes in sexuality for both men and

women is a wonderful idea. this visit is well worth your money because this lack of excitement may have a medical reason.

6. Make time for sex in your marriage even if that is talking, touching, and lying close to one another. sex is not intercourse, although intercourse is part of sex. sex is touching, talking, kissing, and creating intimacy and sharing each other's fantasies. schedule time for being intimate, and take your time.

7. Laugh together. I would never have sex with someone I couldn't laugh with. If you cannot play with your partner during sex, you are going to be bored at some point in your marriage.

Couples may become afraid the first time they begin to feel bored with sex. They question the strength of their marriage if they are bored in the bedroom. However, boredom is something you can work through in a marriage (as are most things) and is never a reason for divorce. Make sure you know who and what you are bored with. *Many times boredom with a partner is boredom with self.* I would question the emotional maturity as well as the character of someone leaving a marriage because of boredom with themselves.

Keeping your love alive with children at home

Studies show that one out of every two marriages will end in divorce. There are many reasons for this, but one of the main reasons is that when things change in the relationship (such as having children) couples forget to adjust and prioritize. Your marriage has to take top priority if you want it to withstand the test of children. When you have children you must let go of the concept of having everything planned. Learn to take advantage of spontaneous times such as nap time. This is a perfect time to leave the dishes in the sink or the dirty laundry. Grab your spouse instead and make the most from your extra moments.

The routine of being a parent can get in the way of spending time with your spouse. When you have a child you begin to work together and most of your day (and night) is consumed with the kids. Soon sex and intimacy may become routine—done in the same room, the same way, or both people are too exhausted to have sex. Try making love in a different room or at a different time when the kids are out of the house. Call your spouse at work and surprise him/her once in a while by flirting again. Date night has to be on your calendar once a week, and try to have at least one weekend away every 4 to 6 weeks.

Couples tend to forget how special their spouses are to them, and taking each other for granted happens in most couples. You don't need to get stuck in this situation though. When you find yourself taking your partner for granted it's time to recognize the fact and do something about it—a favorite meal, dessert, or a kiss and a simple, "what would I do without you?" This makes your partner feel loved and appreciated. Don't wait to receive that special treatment, rather focus on giving it.

Life is about balance and many couples become panicked when they feel as if they are losing the intimacy in their marriage. The most wonderful aspect of this it that it is POSSIBLE TO GET IT BACK! Life presents many occasions in our lives when we are out of balance. Don't scare yourself if you haven't had intimacy for a couple of weeks. Simply sit down with your partner and identify steps you can each take to get it back. Divorce is almost 100% avoidable, but it does take awareness and action on your part.

Research has suggested that more important than sex for a couple's happiness and health is cuddling. Cuddling provides many benefits besides a sense of security and closeness. It also provides stimulus to our olfactory centers (the smell of our partner makes us feel loved) and our touch centers, and it helps to release oxytocin (the feel-good hormone that helps us feel love toward our partner). Cuddling also provides another form of communication that sexual intercourse doesn't. It allows us to feel closer without draining our energy. **Sometimes the best communication happens when couples are holding one another.**

Many times, couples' first homework assignment from me is to begin touching each other more and talking less. When sex isn't going well, not only do you lose that physical connection but you lose the emotional connection too. Often you become more critical of your partner as well as irritable and annoyed. **The emotional connection is much more important than the sexual one, because the emotional connection determines if the sexual one will happen, and how frequently.** Touching and cuddling are the best ways to restore and build the emotional connection. **When couples touch, they let down their guard and begin feeling acceptance and love of their partner.** If cuddling is continued, the feeling of love and connection leads to better communication and sex.

Women may fault men, saying that they don't like to cuddle and that they jump too quickly to sexual intercourse. My experience, as well as reports from the Kinsey Institute for Research in Sex, Gender and Reproduction, suggests this is not true. According to Kinsey's research, among couples in committed relationships, tenderness may be more important to the man than to the woman. Regular kissing and cuddling lead to greater satisfaction in the relationship in men than in their partners, especially as they grow older. When I ask couples to list the number one problem in their relationships, it is the men, not the women, who mention the lack of intimacy. When I question further, they talk about missing the touching, caressing, and soft talking they once shared with their partners.

The time to begin cuddling is early in the relationship. If you have let that go while raising kids, or pursuing demanding careers, you can still get it back. Setting aside a little bit of time into your day to hug or touch your spouse will add a closeness you may have thought was gone forever. You may not need to mention it to your partner. Sometimes their noticing changes in you without your talking about it makes it more special. However, if you have a partner who thinks you only touch him or her when you want sex, then communicating about the benefits of cuddling may be a better option. Reassuring your spouse that it is the intimacy and closeness that you want may be enough to convince your partner to cuddle.

Whenever I ask a person who has lost a spouse what they miss most, I receive many answers, but at the top of many lists is the loss of being held by that person, **the hugs, the way their skin smelled, and how that person's nearness made their body feel.** Stress, illness, and depression can affect sexual performance, but anyone can cuddle. A couple's ability to cuddle, not to perform sex, is one of the best predictors of an emotionally/ physically close, happy, and healthy relationship. Below are a few tips to help you get started with your "cuddle plan."

Cuddle Plan

1   You can cuddle anywhere, which is convenient, but being captive together makes it special. places like airplanes or movie theatres are great places to begin cuddling.

2   No one likes to cuddle on a hard surface, so make sure you have a "cuddle sofa," or overstuffed chair where you both fit comfortably.

3   No one likes to cuddle with a computer on their partner's lap, so get rid of laptops, cell phones, iphones, and ipads.

4   Smoking while cuddling is not wise. Getting burned or the smell of smoke in your face causes coughing and disgust.

5   Talk softly while cuddling.

6   Kissing is not necessary, but is nice while cuddling.

7   Being a good listener while cuddling is also important. your partner will feel more secure and may want to tell you things not said before.

8   Being gentle is part of cuddling.

9   Cuddling has no objective other than to feel close to your partner… so don't rush to finish.

10 Cuddling is helping your partner and you to be healthier with lower blood pressure and respiration. Imagine your ability to heal.

Many articles and commercials address the problems men have about intimacy, but women have intimacy disorders too. Intimacy issues may develop in small children who live in an environment that is not safe. Children who are criticized or believe that their feelings are not respected by their parents may become distrustful and reluctant to share their true identity. They may grow up being fearful of sharing their emotions.

On some level we all have intimacy problems. There is a feeling that you should never put all of your eggs in one basket and that you must never trust anyone completely with your body, ideas, fantasies, or desires. A problem arises when you realize that the person you married doesn't really know you. When you leave and think of them, you cannot recall a time when you shared "real intimacy". Sex becomes a function. And it no longer brings the feeling of familiarity that it once did. If you feel that your relationship is headed in this direction, it is important to talk to your partner about how you are feeling. You may find yourself having to overcome your own reluctance to trust that your spouse will listen to you and not react with anger. To avoid the conversation may mean the death of your marriage.

Problems with intimacy may look like this:

- A spouse works all the time and forgets his/her partner's birthday or anniversary (either one is not good to forget).

- A spouse wants to be taken care of but forgets to express appreciation. A partner no longer holds the loved one in the middle of the night or laughs about "old times," and fails to offer reassurance when needed.

- A spouse finds it uncomfortable to talk about a failure at work because of fear of being misjudged. (If your major complaint is that your spouse won't reveal vulnerability, it may be because when that happens you react negatively to what is revealed).

- A spouse who is jealous of a wife or husband's friend withdraws rather than talk about it.

Tips for restoring intimacy:

1 Make a pact not to use disrespectful words to each other. one couple I worked with actually made a list of inoffensive word substitutes to use when they were angry or frustrated with each other. the couple actually had great fun doing this.

2 Keep sex sacred and focus on the experience rather than the time. sex should feel good for both partners. Couples achieve intimacy by having more eye contact during love making or holding each other. Intimacy, not sex, is the connection.

3   Ask your partner for a list of what makes them feel loved. spouses think they know and tend to make assumptions. What made a partner feel loved at age 28 may not work at the age of 40. Keep a mental list and keep it updated. sometimes emptying the dishwasher, which is such a simple expression of love for you to give, means everything to your spouse.

4   Share your feelings with your spouse—even when you feel like a failure or feel rejected or abandoned. Intimacy has nothing to do with a partner being famous or great. It has everything to do with being real.

Romance

Some of the most popular books on the shelves are romance novels. Women buy them by the millions; yet, I often see couples in my office who have grown apart, have low or no libido, and aren't having sex anymore. Women are the primary purchasers of these books, so I scratch my head in wonder at how they can love books about romance, intimacy, and sex, but no longer want it in their personal lives with their partners. While visiting with couples, I gain more understanding about why and how this is possible. When I ask the couple, "What are you doing to nurture your sex life?" they look confused or stare straight ahead, and it is usually the guy who will offer, "She won't let me near her." She retaliates with, "All you ever want is sex." I've read recently that more and more baby boomers are getting divorced. Couples who have been together since college, raised kids, and fought in-laws together are now separating and divorcing. The reason? There are many, but it comes down to the three I have already mentioned: growing apart, losing their libido, and letting their sex life go. There is a belief for many, especially amongst women, that once you marry, you are married for life. You can let yourself go, begin sharing more with your girlfriends than with your husband, and quit being intimate with him, and they (husbands) will still love you and want romance with you. This is not true. Romance is enhanced by knowledge of your own body and a desire for intimacy. ***Romance in a relationship demands time; it demands be-***

ing open to feeling loved and wanting to love. The number one romance fantasy in most books involves the woman feeling frazzled and her man taking her into his arms; she then submits to being totally pleased. (Note that he usually has clothes on; remember that women like men who emit power, so a suit…or at least shorts). The part the romance novel doesn't mention is that the women in these stories know what pleases them and also are mentally prepared for this encounter. Even if they act surprised in the story, the room is magically candle lit and soft Latin music is playing. The man's timing is always impeccable, which signifies that he is engaged with her; *he knows her, watches her, and is aware.* **Many husbands in real life cannot even find their socks, let alone notice when their woman is giving signals for intimacy.** Around the house they tend to be dressed in grungy t-shirts, and may even need a shower. Often, in fiction, the wife has let herself go and is no longer attractive, but in real life it is just as often the case that the husband has gained weight and begun to pay less attention to his appearance when he is at home.

If your marriage is getting stale and you are becoming distant, you owe it to your family and your spouse to work on closing this gap before it becomes too wide to cross. Reading a romance novel is fine, but your marriage will benefit more if you begin by putting some romance into your real life.

It saddens me to talk to couples who are divorcing because they "grew apart" or no longer want to work on the marriage. They trade partners, leave their children, and destroy their families because they cannot take the loneliness they have co-created with their spouse. They seek another to fill the void and like a miner clutching at fool's gold, they tell themselves they have found the real thing, the love of their life, or their soul mate. The real thing is the love story you are currently working on within your marriage.

STEP 4 GO: FOR BETTER SEX

Having improved communication, addressed issues of health and self-image, and re-energized romance and intimacy, Lilly and Robert are ready to find new ways to better sex. They seem much more comfortable together in our sessions now and generally happier. It hasn't happened over night, but both have lost weight and appear more fit and relaxed. They sit side by side and sometimes share a loving look. The sex they share is part of a stronger, more trusting and informed relationship, and they are ready to explore new ways to please each other sexually. They are well on their way to functioning once again as a couple. Understanding the Big "O"

Women are more complicated sexually than men and the way they achieve orgasm is much different. They need the right mood—the right fantasy, time to relax or to feel sexy and desired, and then they need the right position.

The idea of orgasms and their importance to women's health is talked around but not really talked about. Oprah had someone on her show who specialized in sex and talked about the "sure thing" (a vibrator that is guaranteed to create an orgasm). Many women went out to buy one since it "guaranteed an orgasm". **A number of women came to see me after failing with the vibrator. They had to be told that orgasms are never a sure thing.** If they have a partner they love and who is patient and helpful in satisfying them, that is very close to a "sure thing".

Cardiologists tell us of the health benefits to the heart of one *square of a dark chocolate bar* per day). **One square?** Guess what! Orgasms are also very good for your heart and as far as they (the medical establishment) know, you can have as *many as you want.*

Orgasms can and do help with healing many parts of the body.
Look at this short list just for starters:

- **Pain relief:** Oxytocin, a natural chemical in the body during climax gets some of the credit. A study by Beverly Whipple, a professor emeritus at Rutgers University and a famed sexologist and author, found that when women masturbated to orgasm "the pain tolerance threshold and pain detection threshold increased significantly -- by 74.6 percent and 106.7 percent respectively."

- **Cardio health:** Numerous studies have reported that orgasm lowers blood pressure and may protect us from strokes due to the release of stress during climax.

- **Healing wounds:** Research is being done regarding the ability of orgasm to rejuvenate the body enough to heal wounds quicker. Several studies have shown that the release of oxytocin can help the sores that many diabetics struggle with by regenerating certain cells (this data is still being studied so there are no clear markers of how many orgasms are necessary for healing to take place).

- **Fights aging:** The old saying of use it or lose it really applies here. Maybe it is the closeness, the cuddling, the communication, or the actual orgasm itself, but women who continue to have orgasms report feeling younger and looking younger. The best way to prevent vaginal atrophy is to have more orgasms.

How can a woman learn to have more orgasms?

1. Relax. If you focus too much on achieving an orgasm then it will become that much harder to achieve one. try to enjoy the experience and stay in the present. there is no goal.

2. If something feels good stay there. there is no right or wrong when it comes to your body; do what feels good for you.

3. If you have a loving partner, communicate with him. no guy has a master plan for your orgasm. only you hold the owner's manual.

4. Enjoy yourself. there is nothing sinful about exploring your body and celebrating the beautiful aspects of you. stay away from critiquing your body; learn to appreciate its uniqueness instead of being critical. real bodies are not airbrushed, and they are all slightly different (thank God).

5. Fantasize. fantasy is very important for women in regard to their orgasms. fantasies are yours to use; you do not have to share them,

nor do you have to feel guilty about using them if they help you enjoy sex with your partner.

How a man can help his partner achieve orgasm:

1 Remember the importance of romance, cuddling, and a sensual atmosphere to turn a woman on.

2 Take your time.

3 Hold her the way she likes to be held. many women enjoy having their breasts caressed; others don't. find out. It is time to think of her, not yourself.

4 Women may know where they like to be touched. ask them instead of assuming.

5 Many women use vibrators and other ways to become stimulated. ask to join her with this. When you become defensive in regard to her sexual practices she may feel shame and begin to hide these things from you.

6 Do tell her that she is the most beautiful and sexy woman you know.

Women come in frequently to talk about their sexual health and they should—it's important. In fact, along with healthy eating, exercise, and annual checkups with your physician, sex can help preserve your health and eliminate diseases. What discourages many women from getting the help they need regarding their sexual health is embarrassment or fear of judgment when they talk to their doctor about it. If your doctor cannot handle your questions, find a doctor who can. Sometimes physicians are not comfortable with their own sexuality, and if they aren't comfortable with themselves, they will not be able to be comfortable with you. Resist the idea that it isn't important. It is very important and can make the difference between a healthy, sexy woman and a woman who feels as if those times are gone forever or were never meant for her. All women can have an orgasm and enjoy their sexuality.

An interesting example of the role of culture and the importance of sexual knowledge

A couple whose ethnic families arranged their marriage have been mar-

ried for five years. They have a child who is nearly 3 years old.. The gentleman tells me that he feels as though he loves his wife, but he doesn't desire her as much as she does him. He tells me that before she comes to him he likes her to be in Indian style dress. He also likes her to have make up on and look beautiful. His wife takes offense at this. She doesn't understand this. She and he were both virgins prior to marriage. They are both engineers. She feels that his need to have her look and present herself in a certain way is "weird." She validates her thoughts by saying, "All of my American friends think it's strange too." They all talk about their husbands wanting sex all the time. Mine rarely wants sex, and when he does, it has to be done in a certain manner. Sari has never had an orgasm with sex, and asked me where her clitoris was. When I showed her a diagram she found it helpful, as she had thought it was in the back near the anus.

Masturbation and Vibrators

Masturbation is fun for one, but more fun for two. The only vibrators many of us have seen may be the ones talked about on a TV show or seen on a wild weekend in Vegas. If you have never used a vibrator or introduced one to your partner you are missing out on another aspect of love making. Recent research has suggested that about 50% of both men and women have used a vibrator with a partner at least once. Slightly more men than women agree that vibrators can make sex with a partner more exciting, but for both, the number is close to 60 percent. And we know from other research that about two-thirds of women don't experience orgasm with penetration alone; one way to remedy that is with the use of vibrators.

The first issue for some women is their preconception about vibrators. "If you think of vibrators—or any other part of sex—as 'creepy,' you're showing resistance. Resistance is a product of your own thoughts, which means you can change them and open yourself up to communication and growth. My first request would be that the word "creepy" be changed to "uncomfortable." This opens up a wonderful conversation—if you're uncomfortable with something, you can add something else to lovemaking, and not necessarily all at once. You might not be comfortable with a vibrator, but you might like being massaged during lovemaking with wonderful massage oil. I encourage women—and couples—to try new things, slowly, without rejecting the concept of lovemaking with new items."

"Women are sometimes reluctant to own their own sexuality," and this works against introducing a vibrator—and other things—into a couple's intimacy. Men are so visual with regard to sex that watching a partner masturbate with a vibrator—especially if she is able to enjoy it -- is exciting. Men love watching the woman they love enjoy sex. They also want to please the woman. When the woman is able to allow the man to hold the vibrator for her, or use it gently on him, he begins to see the benefits. He may feel rejected if she prefers the vibrator to him, but including him and showing him what feels best being touched is a big turn-on for men. If she can talk about what feels good, how she likes to be touched, the intimacy will be a thousand times stronger.

Women and Vibrators

How to begin using a vibrator

If you are currently in a relationship, shopping for sex toys can be an exciting adventure and make you feel closer to your partner. Inviting your partner to go along with you makes him or her feel close to you and says that you are open to experimenting. The real focus in introducing a vibrator, or any type of new experience to lovemaking, is not the penis or vagina, but your ability to let go, explore, and broaden your awareness and understanding of your sexual self—and your partner. Being able to express yourself sexually and feeling safe and secure in that relationship heightens your health both physically and emotionally.

Shopping on line is easy and comfortable as it affords you privacy, but you must be open to asking questions. Don't ever buy a product from any web site if the reviews are poor or if you cannot talk to someone about the product. There are very safe web sites, such as **www.middle-sexmd. com,** which focus on sex for those over the age of 35. This site, which is managed by a Gynecologist and a board of medical professionals, is available to help answer your questions. Purchasing products that feel good to your touch and smell good is important. Make sure you ask about these qualities prior to purchase.

When you have purchased your vibrator, familiarized yourself with the way it works, made sure it has no sharp edges or seams and determined whether it is waterproof, you may want to experiment with it a bit. Even if you're planning to use your vibrator with a partner, it's a good idea to check it out by yourself first. You'll feel less self-conscious and you can really concentrate on how it feels. Make sure you have enough time and privacy. Finding the perfect atmosphere to use your vibrator may take experimentation. A lubricant used with your vibrator will help make the experimenting more enjoyable. Play with the lights turned on. Not everyone is comfortable with this suggestion, but I think playing with a vibrator with the lights on can be very educational and useful. You can discover specific places on your body that are rich with nerve endings and ready for enjoyment and stimulation. You can use this information yourself and share with your partner when you're ready.

Get comfortable with the feel of the vibrator on your body. Run it along your body without even turning it on. Notice how it feels. Press it firmly against your skin; press it onto your body and massage your muscles. If the vibrator is made of a hard material, this will probably feel nice. If the vibrator is a soft rubber and doesn't feel smooth against your skin, try it on top of your clothing. This isn't meant to give you an orgasm, but it's a gentle and non-threatening way to introduce your body to the vibrator.

"Move your vibrator from the outside in. Once you turn it on, start by touching the vibrator to your body; this will help you understand the vibration sensation. Even though vibrators are used mostly around the vulva and clitoris, get a feel for the vibration all over your body, including touching the breasts and other areas that feel good. Slowly move to the more sensitive parts of your body.

Don't be in a rush. Explore every part of your body. Vibrators never get tired, and they let you explore every inch of your body for sexual pleasure. Many women find that one side or one part of their clitoris responds to vibration more than another. Move slowly. Leaving a vibrator in place can allow it to establish sensation connections that previously weren't there. Adjust the speed, pressure, and angle of the vibrator. Most vibrators have multiple speed settings; always start on low and work your way up. Experiment with applying different pressure. You may enjoy a lot of deep pressure with clitoral stimulation.

"Most women use vibrators for external stimulation, but as long as your vibrator is safe for it, there's no reason not to try penetration. While far more nerve endings are outside the vagina than inside, lots of women enjoy penetration with a vibrator. A vibrator that is safe for penetration will be smooth, have no rough edges, and won't absorb bodily fluids. Again, start slow and get yourself aroused by using the vibrator externally first.

"There are just two things I caution women about: First, make sure you're using the right lubricant with a vibrator. Silicone-based lubricants will degrade silicone vibrators. And if you're sharing your vibrator outside of a monogamous relationship, put a condom on it.

Men and Vibrators

Men can be aroused with a vibrator too. Their partners can add to their pleasure by adjusting the setting to the lowest, slowest selection and gently moving the vibrator in a slight circular motion over the perineal area. The area behind the testicles and in front of the anus is very sensitive to touch. Pressure here can please a man because of the presence of many nerve endings. A reassuring partner may be required, as many men are reluctant to try a vibrator for their own pleasure. However if partners keep an attitude of openness and enthusiasm, both will benefit. Kissing his neck, lips, or other sensitive areas can be a type of foreplay as well as part of love making. Couples who are open to exploring each other sexually have a more vibrant and close love making experience than those who limit themselves and their partners.

Men, like women, should be asked what they like. A vibrator can stimulate many areas of a man just as it does a woman. Men are especially sensitive in the inner thigh area, around the genitals, and the neck and chest area. Stimulation with a vibrator directly on the penis head or testicles may be too harsh, so go slowly and let him guide.

Some suggestions for being a better lover.

Foreplay is important in all sex and love making for couples. If a man has a small penis or is worried that it is small, foreplay can change him from a so-so lover to an exceptional lover no matter what his penis size. Women respond to clitoral stimulation and enjoy kissing as well as light bites on the neck area during foreplay. Men concerned about their penis size can focus on foreplay that will help please her more, and also help boost his confidence. The majority of women can achieve an orgasm with manual or oral stimulation to the clitoris, and that will reduce the importance of the size of a man's penis if he is concerned with its ability to bring her to orgasm.

Men who are more open to other options for pleasing their partners also seem to suffer less with thoughts of having a "too small penis." Exploring and experimenting with positions is also a good idea. Positions in which the woman is on top so she can control thrusts as well as penetration seem to work best not only for a shorter penis but for better orgasms for women. Always remember the value of pillows. They help position as well as provide comfort. Most women respond positively to their partners' being concerned about comfort during lovemaking.

Positions to experiment with:

- Doggie style works exceptionally well for men with a small penis. The trick is to make sure your partner is comfortable with her head and arms well elevated on a pillow. Placing a pillow under her stomach to help elevate her buttocks in the air helps with penetration. Being able to penetrate this way frees your hands to still touch and caress her, but also will reduce the anxiety of looking at her face for cues that you may not be adequate.

- Your partner may also enjoy the missionary position with a slight modification. Raising her buttocks with pillows while also having her legs open or knees into her shoulders will help open her vagina so you can penetrate. This feels exceptionally close for both partners and both partners can easily be brought to orgasm.

Couples who must deal with a physical flaw, such as a small penis, often seem to have closer relationships than many in the general public. This is because communication is enhanced when one partner feels insecure about a body part and trusts and loves the other enough to talk about it. This is why men who have a small penis or fear of having a small penis are encouraged to work with a therapist or a support group to help facilitate their communication about their issue. The penis size may or may not change, but their ability to communicate about their feelings regarding their penis is what will make a sexual relationship close.

Tips for a Better Sex Life

1. Start to feel good about sex. the brain is the largest sex organ. If you are feeling anxious or are angry at a partner you have to deal with the brain first. Anger that is held in does not create good sex, nor does it help you feel sexy.

2. Ladies, embrace yourselves—your attitude is important. you don't need to be a perfect size. If you have curves and hips embrace them. this is one of the most beautiful aspects of women. most of us have flaws, cellulite, acne, or wrinkles. These "flaws" will not distract from a beautiful smile or a warm embrace.

3. Fantasize. the more you think about sex the more you will want it, so be sure to take time to think about it. do whatever gets you in the mood or makes you feel sexy.

4. Get to know your body. touch yourself so you know the sensitive areas of your body. Where does it make you feel good to touch? do you get goose bumps when you touch a place on your neck or thigh? this knowledge is very important and helpful to the person loving you.

5. Take time for foreplay. the name tells you what it is for. Remind your partner that foreplay starts first thing in the morning and lasts all day. maybe your partner can empty the dishwasher, put the kids to bed, go over homework, or make the dental appointment. your partner cannot read your mind so speak up when and where you need help.

6. Try something new.

7. Tell your partner what you need to make you feel sexy and sensual.

8. Take time to be sensual. don't hurry. pamper yourself. you must love yourself to love another.

9. Watch movies or read books that make you feel sexual. many women find sexual pleasure after reading a romance novel or watching a romantic love story.

10. Invest in massage oils, toys or anything that makes you feel sexy.

Special Couples with Special Issues

You and your partner may enjoy remarkable intimacy and great sex, but some things are beyond your control. You never know when life will throw you a curve. One of the challenges I see frequently is the challenge of living with Cancer. Diagnosis is frightening and treatment may be complex. As the treatment plan is better understood and treatments are received on a schedule, patients can begin to relax a bit, and this usually is when the couple comes to me for help. Cancer changes the partner as well as the patient. When couples embrace, they must deal with both physical and emotional changes. They may have to learn new ways to express their love. The stronger their relationship and the better their communication, the more likely they are to be successful in making necessary adjustments. Below is a case study of just such a couple.

I met Jean and Dan when Jean was 38 years old and Dan was 36. They had children in elementary school, and a new diagnosis of breast cancer. They always shared the cancer, meaning that when they first came in they came together and talked about "Our Cancer." Jean had a very aggressive form of breast cancer, and therefore needed surgery as well as chemotherapy. The treatments caused her to tire easily and she was having difficulty with the removal of her breast. At one point she refused to let Dan see the scar, but after several therapy sessions she became more understanding of what this was doing to Dan. Dan revealed that he had felt the loss of her breast very significantly. Not because he loved the breast so much, but because he knew that Jean valued her breasts as a very significant part of her feminity. He struggled to help her with her loss, and held her when she withdrew from sex. During the treatments they found other ways to connect besides intercourse. Sometimes simply holding one another close while nude helped both of them feel connected and less alone. They were such phenomenal people that when treatment ended and Jean was able to feel like a whole woman again, she began to consider having breast implants, and once again Dan was there to support her, but left the decision totally up to her. She felt loved.

Jean went on to be cancer free and sent me Christmas cards each year with updates about the children. Six years after Jean's breast cancer, I saw Jean and Dan on my client list again. I thought maybe they were in town and just catching up, but unfortunately this was not the case. Jean had just been diagnosed with colon cancer. Even though she and Dan had been down the rocky road of breast cancer, nothing had prepared them for this. Once again, Dan was at her side. This time, they would have to prepare for a colostomy bag and the changes that would make in their sex life. They understood that whatever had to be faced would be easier if they both joined in the treatment and therapy. They did make it through the cancer and the therapy, and their marriage is stronger now than it has ever been. When I asked Dan what his best advice to others would be, he said, "When you love someone there are many ways to connect and feel sexual with them." "Thinking love making is only intercourse is short-sighted and less thrilling than what Cancer has taught Jean and me." —D&

Cancer cannot steal your relationship; it can make it rocky and scary, but it can also deepen it, and make it better than it was before.

Sex and Cancer or Chronic Illness

For both men and women the occurrence of cancer affects every area of their lives, including intimacy with a partner. Fear, anger, questions of "What is happening to me?" or " Why is this happening to me?" are just the beginning. People worry about the effect of their inability to enjoy sex and what this will do to their partner's need for sex, and they feel sad for having lost this bond. Many patients talk about guilt at this time. If there was an affair in their past or some other wrong they feel wasn't resolved, it may be brought up in regard to their sex lives.

Cancer is first attacked on the medical front, but once the patient has completed the necessary surgery or medical treatment, the aid to healing afforded by a caring partner cannot be underestimated. That is why healthcare givers encourage couples to take a stance and survive "Cancer" as a team. When the affected spouse is certain of a partner's support, he or she is more willing to endure the treatment and after care. For these couples, acting as a team will allow them to keep their sex lives open to the changes that may have to be made in their lives. Whether it is prostate, breast, colon, or some other kind of cancer, the couple probably will have to express their intimacy differently. Chemotherapy is exhausting, but holding hands sitting in a bathtub of warm water and good-smelling bath bubbles while relaxing with while relaxing with a partner can provide a deep connection and eroticism that might not have been expected.

There are ways to make love during and after cancer treatment. And, once patients get their energy back and are cancer free, they may find their love making has grown even more pleasurable.

> ## Tips for couples dealing with cancer
>
> 1. take mini vacations:
>   - have lunch for two outside in nice weather.
>   - have movie night at home with a bowl of popcorn or a plate of light foods (While undergoing chemotherapy patients may be nervous about being around a lot of people). staying in with the person you love most provides security and a deep sense of being cared for.
>   - because the human touch is healing, offer your partner a massage as a "get away vacation"
> 2. **read to your partner:** read books such as romance novels, erotica, or a classic love story. during chemotherapy, and sometimes for a short time afterward, vision may be affected. having someone you love read to you is intimate and loving. your partner's voice is actually proven to heal. It slows the respiration and heartbeat of a significant other.
> 3. **reassure your partner:** this is a perfect time to reassure your partner that you love him or her and that you love your sex life. a colostomy bag changes love making forever, but patients who have a willing partner to work with handle the adjustment much better. men who have had a total prostatectomy may have trouble keeping an erection but engaging in oral sex, and seeking treatment such as a penile implant can improve their sex lives. a partner's enthusiasm will help the patient deal with the grief of the loss. a mastectomy is devastating to most women, but if they are with a loving partner they can recover and may explore a wider array of options.

Recovering Sexual Function after Prostate Cancer

Following a radical prostatectomy (surgery to remove the prostate because of cancer), approximately 30% of patients have erectile dysfunction related to reduced blood flow or nerve injury. Although the penile nerves may be preserved during a radical prostatectomy, the majority of men suffer from a temporary nerve paralysis, which may last from months to years. Nerve injury can also lead to penile scarring.

In the past, men were given Viagra and asked to return in a year so their progress in achieving erections could be assessed. This was wrong. Men should be reminded that the penis is a muscle and should be exercised just like any other muscle in the body. If your arm were in a cast for a year you would have muscle wasting and the arm would be weak when you took the cast off. The same concept of "use it or lose it" also applies to the penis. Thus we now ask patients to start exercising the penis immediately after surgery. This is called penile rehabilitation. The goal of penile rehabilitation is to increase blood flow and oxygen to the penile tissue and thus prevent scarring and permanent damage. It is important to take this proactive approach because many times the scarring that occurs in the penis after a radical prostatectomy is irreversible.

There are many medications that can be used to prevent penile scarring and exercise the penis. Viagra 25mg every night has been very effective in preserving erectile function. In one study, men taking 25mg of Viagra every night for 48 weeks after a bilateral nerve sparing radical prostatectomy were almost 7 times more likely to have spontaneous erections than men taking placebo. In addition to nightly dosing of Viagra, MUSE (Medicate Urethral System for Erections) therapy also has been effective in preserving penile function. MUSE is a small medicated pellet which is placed into the urethra and causes dilation of penile blood vessels. Another possibility is testosterone replacement therapy. In one study, approximately 17% of men had low testosterone levels after a radical prostatectomy. Testosterone is responsible for increasing a man's libido and improving penile nerve conduction, and can help certain men maintain their erections. Finally, some men may go on to penile injection therapy in order to achieve erections sufficient for intercourse. This involves inserting a small needle into the side of the penis and injection of medication that increases the blood flow into the penis. Also, the use of a vacuum erection device (VED) on a daily basis has been shown to increase blood flow and oxygen to the penis as well as preserve penile length.

One of the best ways to improve these patients' erections and their compliance with the penile rehabilitation program is to improve their partners' desire for sex. We recently published a paper showing that the men who had the best erections after prostate cancer surgery were those men whose wives had a strong sex drive. This makes sense because single men or those whose wives who are not interested in sex are less likely to have any incentive to do work to achieve erections. Men whose wives are more interested in sex tend to recover faster. This is why we include the female partners of men who undergo a radical prostatectomy in our treatment plan. By including the female partner, we are actually treating the patient.

If medical therapy is ineffective, men have the option of a penile prosthesis. This device, invented at Baylor College of Medicine, revolutionized the treatment of erectile dysfunction. Satisfaction rates have been greater than 95% from both the male patients and their partners.

The psychological impact of a radical prostatectomy on a patient can hardly be overestimated. Imagine a 50-year-old man learning on the day after surgery that he may not ever be able to have sex naturally with his wife again. This can have a devastating impact on the patient and also on his wife. In fact, many men start to experience ED once they receive the diagnosis of prostate cancer. This is why sex therapy plays such an important role in the recovery of sexual function after prostate cancer treatment.

Reinventing Your Relationship In The Face Of Chronic Illness

"It takes a really big man to love a really big scar" –Carly Simon

Nine years as an intimacy and sex counselor for cancer patients taught me more than any textbook or class. I celebrated their success with them, prayed for their healing with them, and sat by their bedside with their loved one when they took their last breaths. Many people would call that a depressing job, but I never lived as fully as when I worked with that population.

One of the many things I learned was that when you have a chronic illness, such as cancer, MS, or depression, your relationships have to change. Intimacy and sex with your partner have to be discussed openly along with emotions such as fear, anger, guilt, and confusion. Sharing these feelings and concerns with your partner can actually move you closer to your partner than ever before. Infertility, impotence, a colostomy bag, the loss of a breast, or the inability to feel or move your legs will contribute to feelings of being only half a person. The scars of the disease on the outside are many times minor compared to the scars left inside. It takes a loving partner to understand that illness is a temporary detour where adjustments need to be made in the way you express your love. Completely withdrawing love or affection can lead to depression or feelings of hopelessness.

Couples need to be better educated about how to express their intimacy and love when a partner becomes ill. Sex is something that should never be avoided between partners, healthy or not. All humans enjoy and need intimacy to feel healthy and loved. These feelings help overcome the obstacles that chronic illness often inflicts.

Here are some suggestions for couples dealing with a chronic illness. As you become more confident in your ability to express your feelings of love to your partner, you are encouraged to seek continued counseling with a therapist.

- **Share the diagnosis.** Talk to your spouse. Remind your partner that you are a team. Anything that affects the wellbeing of one will affect both. This makes the "patient" (your spouse) feel loved and more confident about being able to endure the illness. It also provides an opportunity for you to help with routine care that may be necessary during this time.

- • **Intimacy takes only minutes.** Rather than thinking about a vacation or getaway, take advantage of "mini vacations." These are moments that you can be close by holding hands, watching a funny movie, cuddling on the sofa, listening to old songs together or talking to one another. Many times, these are **"miracle moments"** that life's busy pace robbed from you prior to the illness.

- **Rediscover the joys of "petting."** With chronic illness, skin sensations change. Chemotherapy, for example, can heighten sensitivity of the skin, whereas M.S. can deaden it. Learning to touch one another again without a goal and talking about how that feels can make you feel like a kid again. In a sense, chronic illness makes anyone who endures it an unfamiliar person. Take time to rediscover and allow your partner to set the pace.

- **Start in the tub or shower.** Most of us are comfortable in warm water as it relaxes us and takes some of our pain away. Sitting in the tub with the one you love is an opportunity to relax, look into each other's eyes, and talk. Washing each other's back or feet is also a wonderful way to express your love and develop greater intimacy with your partner. Many times, it is in the intimate setting of a bath that partners are permitted to see and touch the scar. **Your reaction will mean everything, and the best reaction is to thank your partner for showing the scar to you. It is a time to offer assurance that the scar makes you love them more.**

- **Medicate before having sex.** When couples want to share intimacy and sex, it is important that it is planned. This is necessary because pain is often part of a chronic illness. No one in pain feels sexy, so planning your medication at least one hour prior to engaging in sex will help to insure your comfort and ability to enjoy the expression of intimacy.

The loss of a breast, body part, or one's mobility is symbolic of a loss of independence and sometimes of identity. A partner has incredible influence at this time. *In fact, the partner is often the one who is best able to influence how a spouse handles a chronic illness.* **No one wants a partner to suffer from chronic illness, but if that happens, remind yourself that you and you alone may provide the emotional healing your partner needs in order to reclaim his or her sexual and intimate self.**

Some Final Thoughts

TV sex is not real sex. Nor is the sex you see on the internet or IP-HONES. Real sex is the stuff that happens when you care for someone, and holding that person's hand makes you feel special and loved. Real sex is the kind that happens in the bedroom when the kids are upstairs napping, or on a Sunday afternoon during half time. It's the kind that builds with a relationship of trust and caring Evaluating your relationship by reading this book is an opportunity to grow. You know what didn't work, and you know what sometimes worked, so it's time to prepare to get your relationship back on track or get on with your life without that partner. We spend a lot of money and time buying our gym memberships and cookbooks to get our body in shape, but we forget that our relationship needs a plan too. Your relationship can be neglected in a variety of ways. Letting your body go or using food, cigarettes, alcohol or drugs to manage chronic stress all affect how we relate to ourselves as well as our partners. We are bombarded with ads for losing weight and new healthy foods to try, as well as new exercise workouts. **The best workout for your relationship and the quickest way to feel connected and encouraged in your relationship is to have sex with your partner.** Not only that, every cell in your body responds in a positive way when you have sex in a committed, healthy relationship. **Couples who have sex are healthier, more connected, and less depressed.** What drug could offer you all of that and more?

Table 1: Signs and Symptoms of Low Testosterone

Physical Signs	Symptoms
• Increased body fat, BMI • Reduced muscle bulk and strength • Low bone mineral density • Loss of body hair	• Decreased energy or motivation • Diminished libido (Erectile dysfunction in men) • Dimiished work performance • Poor concentration and memory • Sleep disturbance • Depression

Figure 1
Modified from: Female Sexual Response: The Role of Drugs in the Management of Sexual Dysfunction.
Basson, Rosemary; MB, BS
Obstetrics & Gynecology. 98(2):350-353, August 2001.

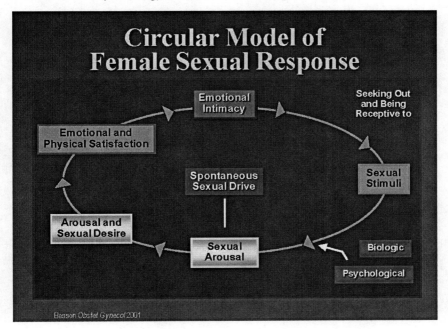

Figure 2 Female urinary/reproductive system

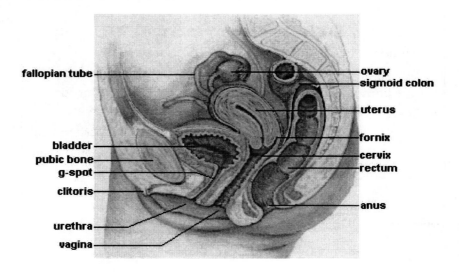

fallopian tube — ovary — sigmoid colon — uterus — bladder — pubic bone — g-spot — clitoris — fornix — cervix — rectum — anus — urethra — vagina

Figure 3 Male urinary/reproductive system

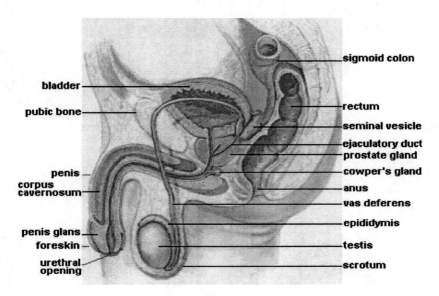

APPENDICES

APPENDIX 1
PHQ-9 Patient Depression Questionnaire

PATIENT HEALTH QUESTIONNAIRE-9 (PHQ-9)

Over the last 2 weeks, how often have you been bothered by any of the following problems? (Use "✔" to indicate your answer)	Not at all	Several days	More than half the days	Nearly every day
1. Little interest or pleasure in doing things	0	1	2	3
2. Feeling down, depressed, or hopeless	0	1	2	3
3. Trouble falling or staying asleep, or sleeping too much	0	1	2	3
4. Feeling tired or having little energy	0	1	2	3
5. Poor appetite or overeating	0	1	2	3
6. Feeling bad about yourself — or that you are a failure or have let yourself or your family down	0	1	2	3
7. Trouble concentrating on things, such as reading the newspaper or watching television	0	1	2	3
8. Moving or speaking so slowly that other people could have noticed? Or the opposite — being so fidgety or restless that you have been moving around a lot more than usual	0	1	2	3
9. Thoughts that you would be better off dead or of hurting yourself in some way	0	1	2	3

FOR OFFICE CODING __0__ + _____ + _____ + _____

=Total Score: _____

If you checked off any problems, how difficult have these problems made it for you to do your work, take care of things at home, or get along with other people?

Not difficult at all	Somewhat difficult	Very difficult	Extremely difficult
☐	☐	☐	☐

Developed by Drs. Robert L. Spitzer, Janet B.W. Williams, Kurt Kroenke and colleagues, with an educational grant from Pfizer Inc. No permission required to reproduce, translate, display or distribute.

APPENDIX 2

Answering questionnaires may provide helpful insights, and might be useful to take to the doctor with you.

PHQ9 (Patient Health Quesionnaire -9)

http://phqscreeners.com/pdfs/02_PHQ-9/English.pdf

ADAM (Androgen Deficiency in the Aging Male)

http://www.counseling-office.com/surveys/test_testosterone_deficiency.phtml

SHIM (Sexual Health Inventory for Males)

http://www.njurology.com/_forms/shim.pdf

DSDS (Decrease in Sexual Desire Screener

http://www.omniaeducation.com/whav/WHAV_Addenda2/
Decreased_Sexual_Desire_Screener_DSDS_Female_Sexual_
Dysfunction_Tool.pdf

FSFI (Female Sexual Function Index)

http://www.obgynalliance.com/files/fsd/FSFI_Pocketcard.pdf

CPSIA information can be obtained
at www.ICGtesting.com
Printed in the USA
FSOW02n1413020916
24460FS

9 781628 651829